CRE8IVES BE A DREAM ACHIEVER

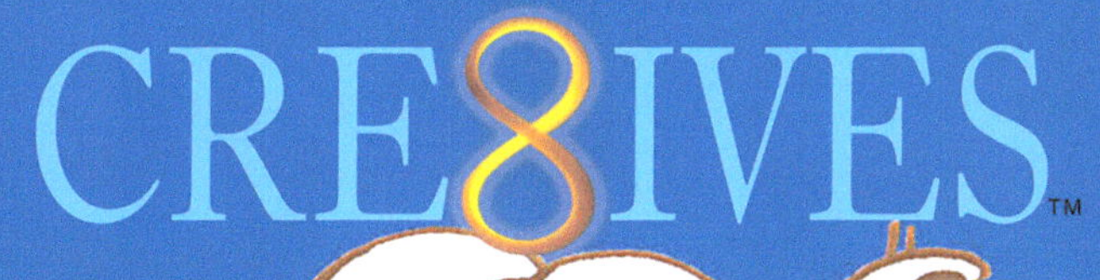

BE A DREAM-ACHIEVER™

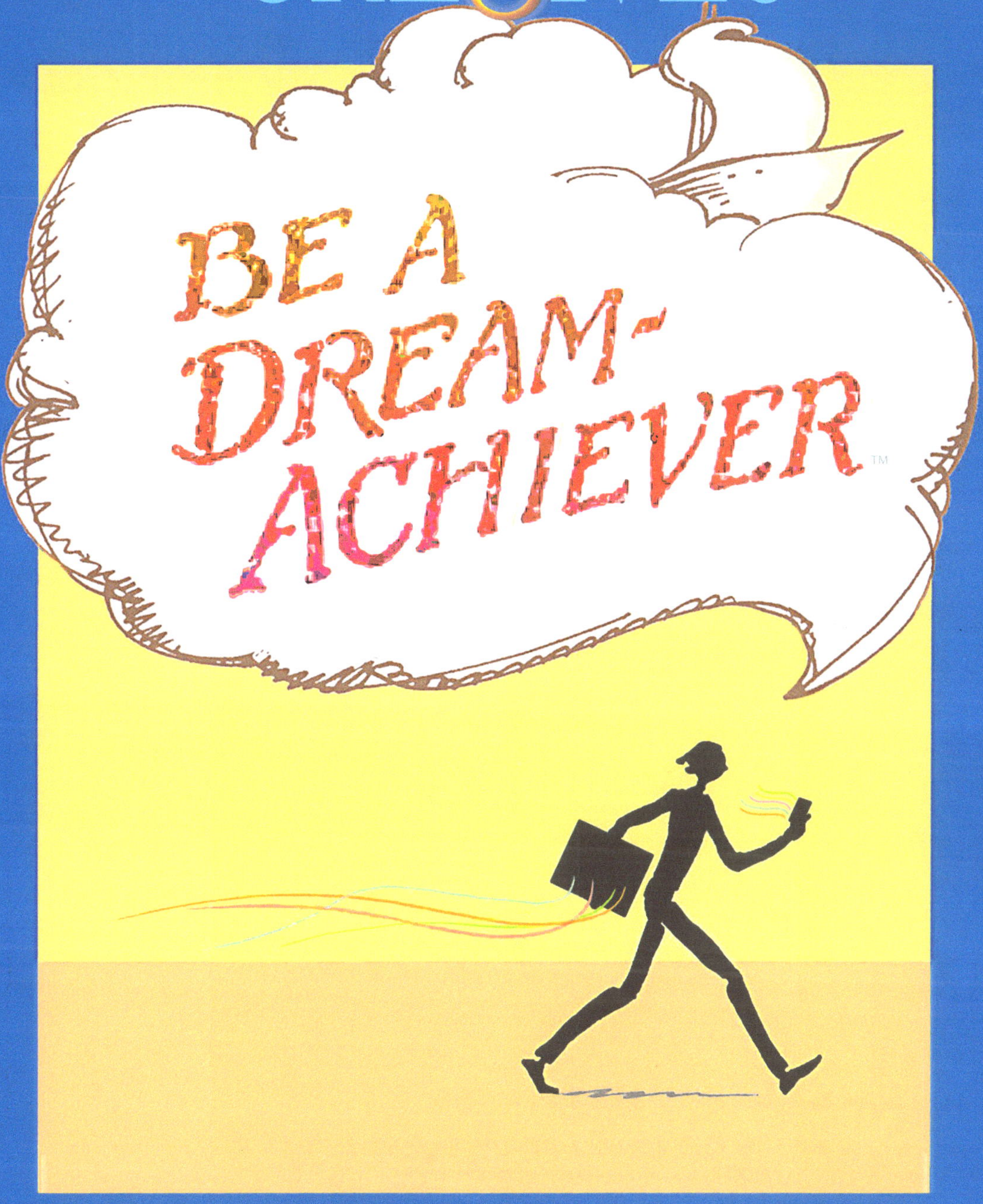

THE ART OF CAREER SUCCESS

XULON PRESS

Xulon Press
2301 Lucien Way #415
Maitland, FL 32751
407.339.4217
www.xulonpress.com

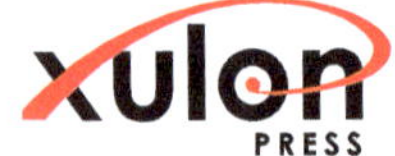

ARTISTS: Nancy Mckarney, Warren Dayton, Robert Hover, Shutterstock

FRONT AND BACK COVER: Warren Dayton, design@artifactink.com

Paperback ISBN-13: 978-1-66286-746-0

Dedication

LIFE IS A SPECIAL OCCASION. THE BE A DREAM ACHIEVER WORKBOOK IS DEDICATED TO YOU. YOU MATTER.

Believe in yourself and in the power, you have to control your own life, day by day. Believe in the strength that you have deep inside, and your faith will help show you the way. Believe in tomorrow and what it will bring.

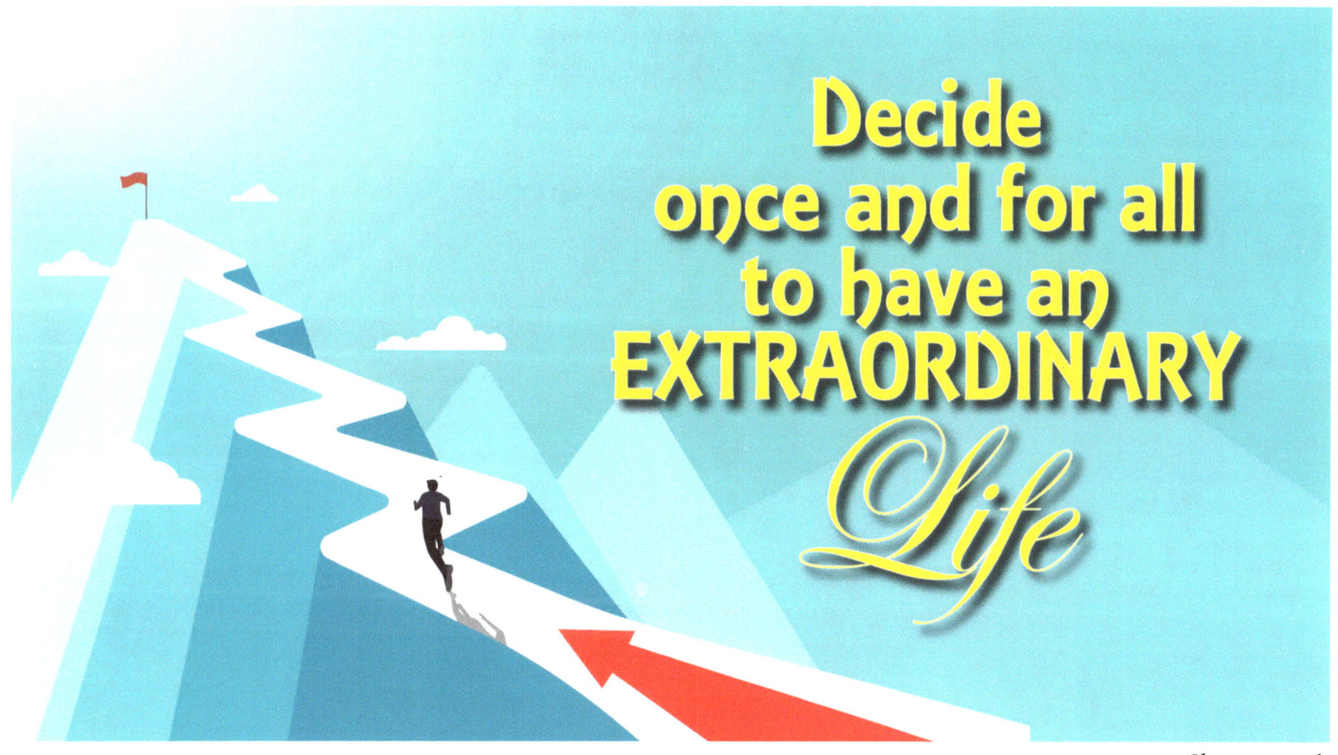

Shutterstock

Dream big, be awesome. Once you have committed yourself to your dream, there is no telling what you will be able to achieve, no matter what stage of life you are in. Dream with your heart, and love with your soul. Be strong and enjoy the journey.

TABLE OF CONTENTS

As you delve into **THE ART OF CAREER SUCCESS WORKBOOK** keep in mind,
"A PICTURE IS WORTH A 1,000 WORDS". — *Terry Sheppard*

PROLOGUE

Chapter 1

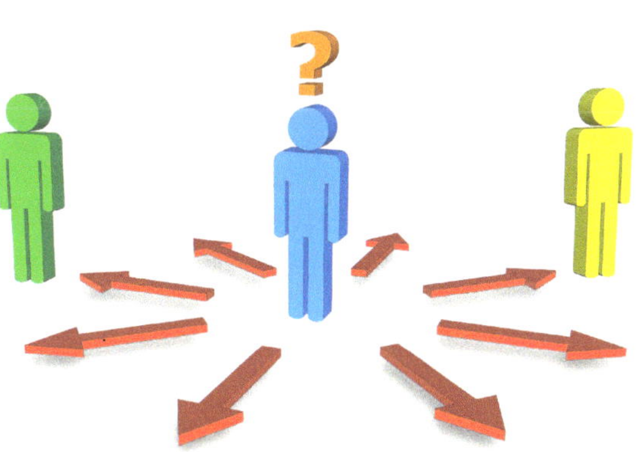

Chapter 2

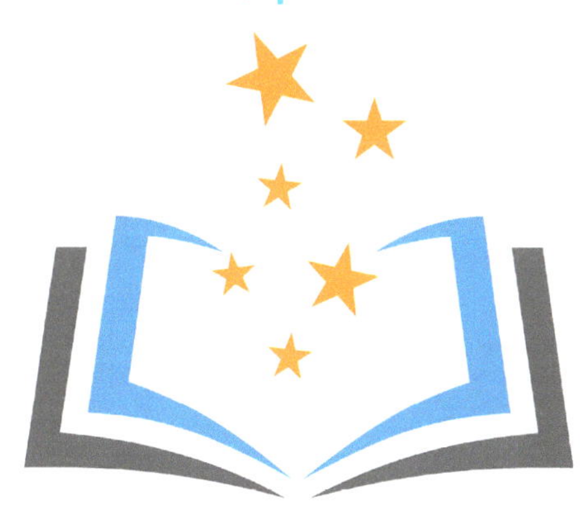

Chapter 3

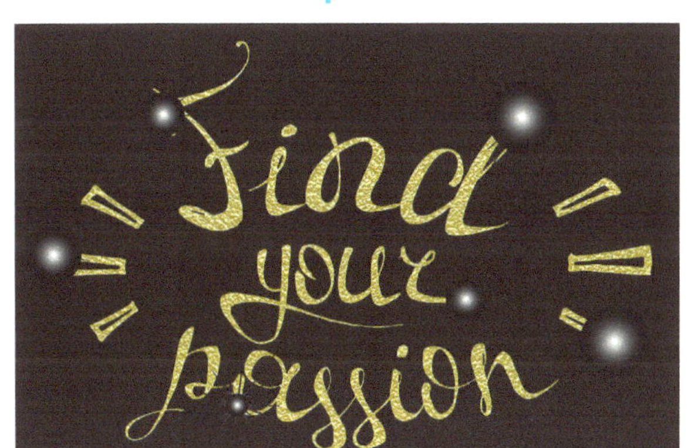

Chapter 4

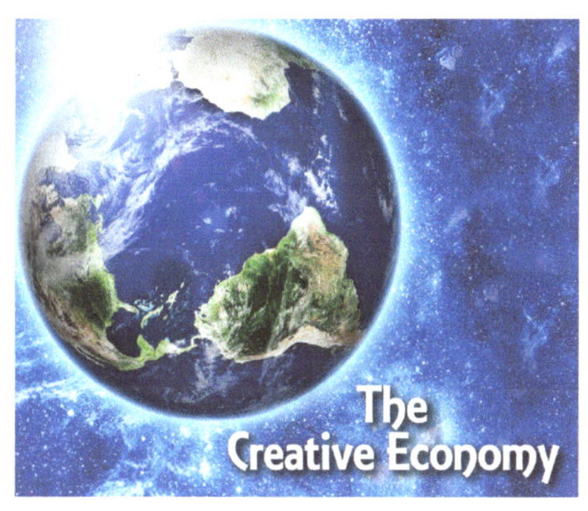

Chapter 5

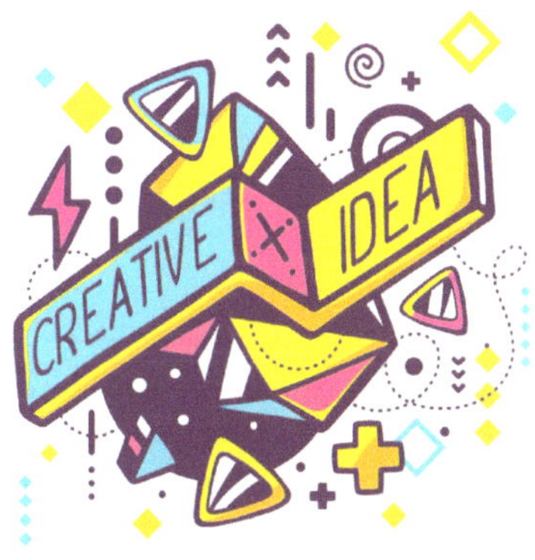

Chapter 6

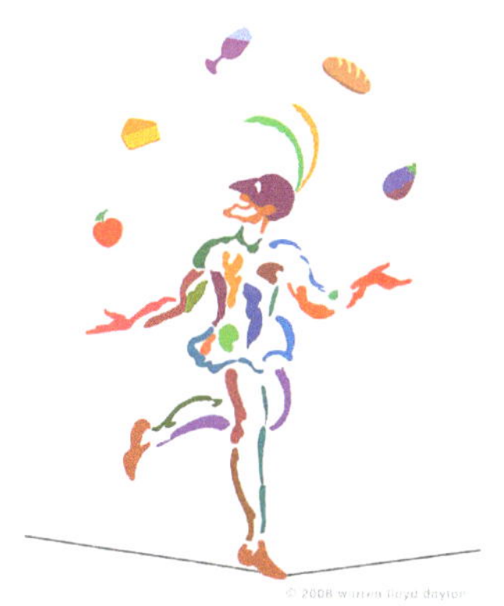

Chapter 7

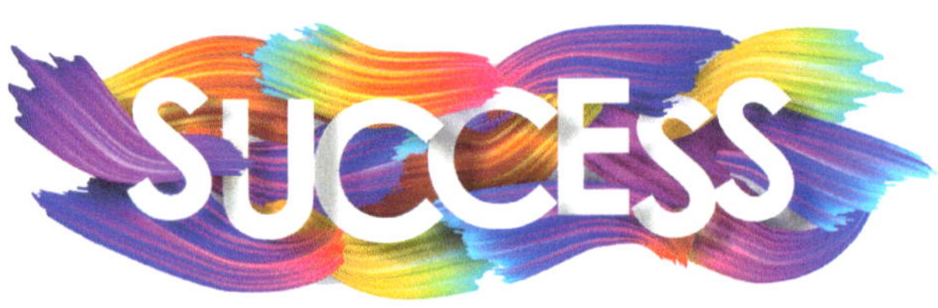

Chapter 8

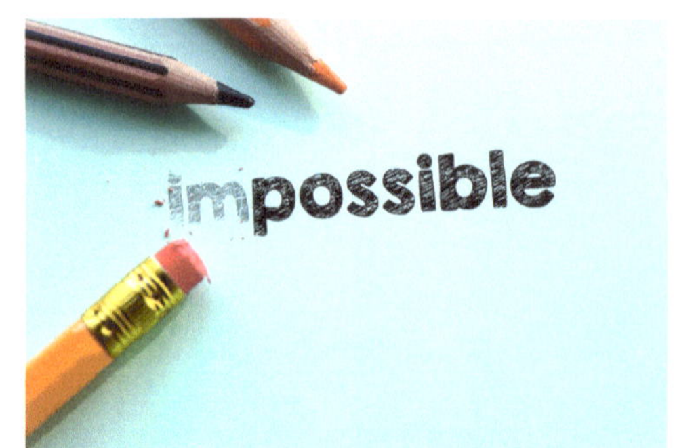

Chapter 9

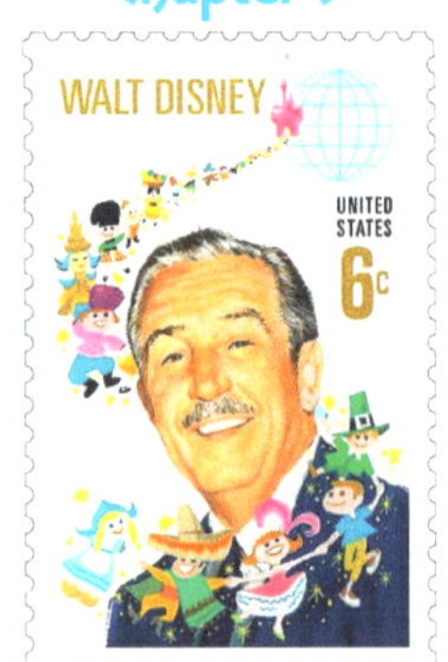

Chapter 10

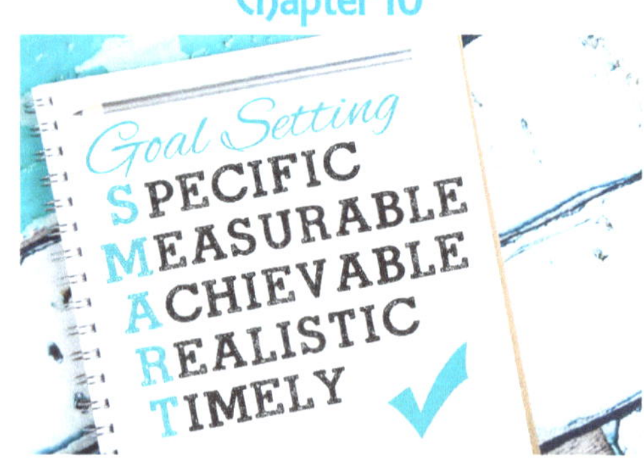

Chapter 11

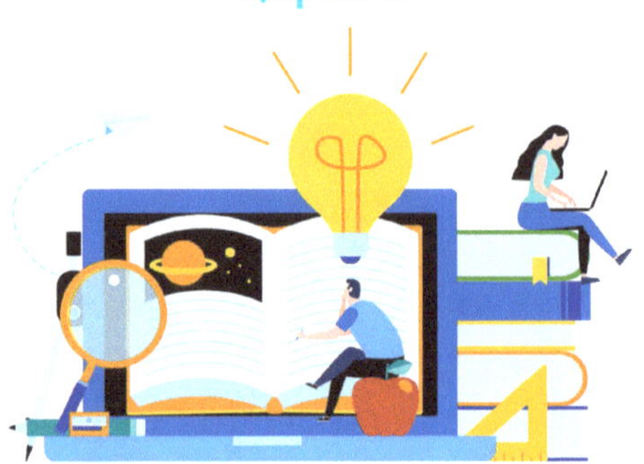

Chapter 12

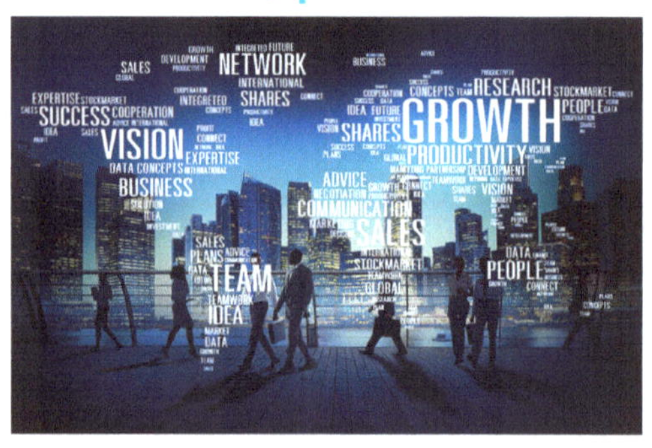

Chapter 13

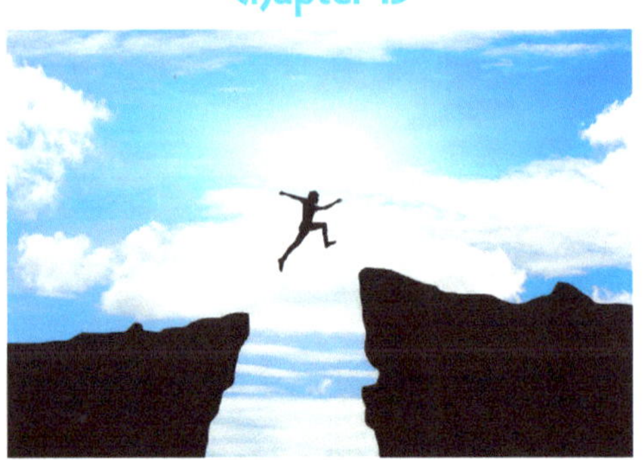

Chapter 14

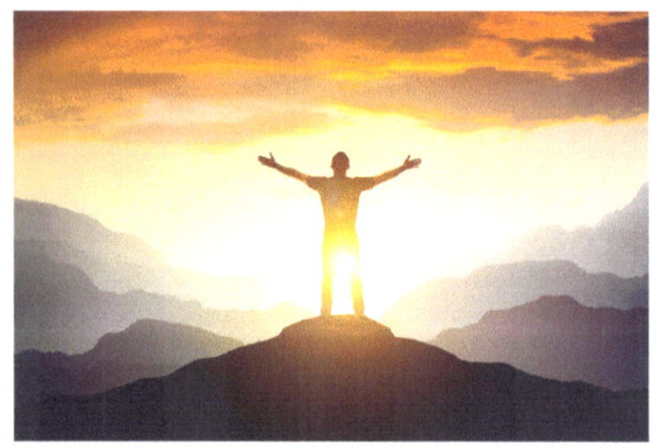

EPILOGUE

Prologue

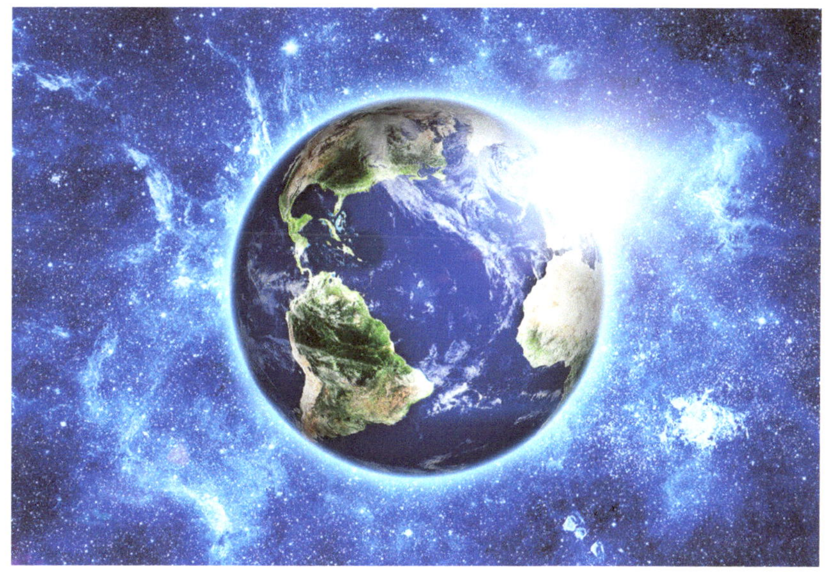

Shutterstock

E   ART   H

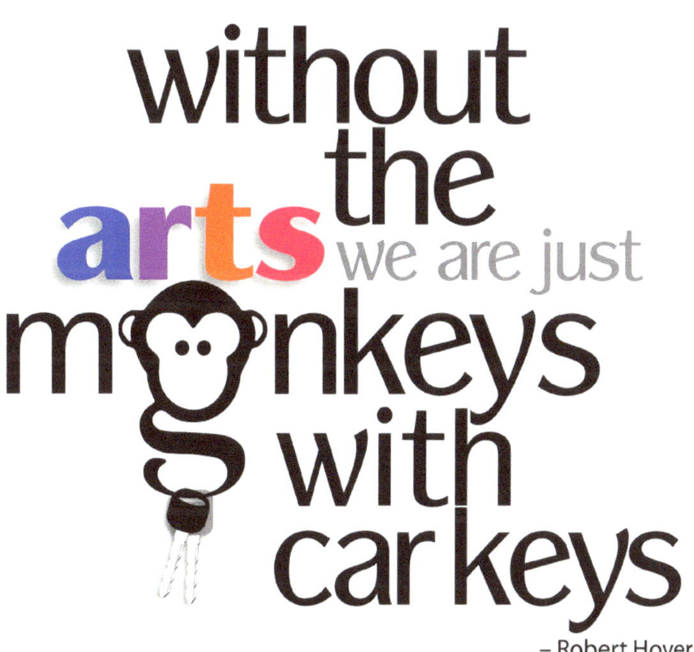

– Robert Hover

Do you have a dream of a life of passion in the creative arts, achieving personal and career success, and making a living? *Talent alone is never enough.* ***CRE8IVES: BE A DREAM ACHIEVER WORKBOOK*** is a life-map for anyone in the arts. Become who you were born to be. Life is a special occasion, and you are special.

CRE8IVES™

Art Directors	Motion Picture Producers & Directors
Craft Artists	Film & Video Editors
Fine Artists Including Painters, Sculptors Illustrators	Digital Artists
Folk Artists	Actors
Hobby Artists	Dancers
Multi-Media Artists	Choreographers
Animators	Sheer Design
Commercial & Industrial Designers	Music Directors
Architects	Musicians & Announcers
Landscape Architects	Reporters & Correspondents
Fashion Designers	Writers and Authors
Culinary Arts	Media & Communication Workers
Floral Designers	Public Relations Specialists
Graphic Designers	Photographers
Interior Designers	Education Training & Library Occupation
Merchandise Display	Art, Drama, & Music Teachers Postsecondary
Window Trimmers	Self-Enrichment Education
Set & Exhibit Designers	
Entrepreneurs	

Art and Culture are important parts of the human experience. They say art is is subjective — so what is it in the eye of the planner? And how is Culture seen with that same eye? From the first drawings scratched onto cave walls and the first stories told around campfires in the long-ago, Art and Culture have been important parts of the human experience. Talent enthralls us. We are overcome by the significance of Monet's paintings, captivated by Celine Dion's endearing voice, and gripped by the motion-picture performance of Al Pacino. However, we live in a world of upsets. The most talented do not always end up as celebrities, and those with less talent often do. Astonishing conclusions are written into our history and occur around us every day. For example, Morley Safer, best known for his long tenure on the CBS network news magazine *60 Minutes,* profiled the life of the self-proclaimed "Painter of Light," Thomas Kinkade. Safer concluded his documentary profile on Kinkade stating that Kinkade was the world's most collected painter.

Have you ever studied a very popular, commercially successful creative artist's work and said to yourself or someone else that this artist's work is mediocre at best? Why are the most talented not always the best? Why is it that some creatives in the arts of unexceptional talent and skill, regardless of the discipline, become famous and financially successful? What enables the less skilled to be at times far more successful? How many creative artists with great talent do you know, who go unrecognized, struggling to scratch out a living for themselves and their families?

There is no proxy for talent, but there are numerous augmentations that can transfigure even modest talent into greatness. *Perfectionism, initiative, passion, and fortitude* are examples of behaviors that award talent with success and drive ordinary skill sets into an extraordinary success story. These four qualities are not all-inclusive; they are among the most important traits that do not rely on talent. The ***CRE8IVES: BE A DREAM ACHIEVER WORKBOOK*** doesn't diminish talent but amplifies the performance that can go together with it to build day-by-day a life dream and career success. This workbook is designed to help you blend creative vision with business confidence to develop the career you love and create a plan for growth to succeed in enterprise. This workbook is a how-to offering of timeless principles used by successful men and women throughout history.

"If we did all the things, we are capable of doing, we would literally astound ourselves."
–Thomas A. Edison

For centuries, creative arts and business have been intertwined. In our contemporary culture, there are even more opportunities for enterprise. The aim of ***CRE8IVES: BE A DREAM ACHIEVER WORKBOOK*** is to provide you with the knowledge and skills to increase your dream life in the global arts community and cultural age. The good ole days are gone forever. The world has moved on. In the Global Village economy, competition is staggering for every dollar spent on art and entertainment. It is one thing to be a creative today, quite another to market and sell your talent. Talent alone no longer provides the platform to succeed in the arts and make a modest livelihood. In our future world, an artist must have business savvy and know how to market themselves and their talent.

To succeed and sustain success in the creative arts enterprises today requires comprehension of the conventional industry economy of production, distribution, and consumption. The ***CRE8IVES: BE A DREAM ACHIEVER WORKBOOK*** showcases genuine business practices like planning, finance, marketing, developing consistent work habits, knowledge of business structures, and industry/business organizational behavior and management. The content of this workbook is not pie-in-the-sky fluff. It is down-to-earth, rock solid, proven business concepts that will help you make your creative life dream come true. These entrepreneurial spirit and business strategies can help you develop the creative work you love for career growth and/or succeed as a business in an enterprise in your chosen field. Whether you're an emerging, mid-career, or seasoned artist, you will learn how to take control of your career by becoming your own business manager and strategic marketer.

"If a person has a talent and cannot use it, they have failed. If they have a talent and use only half of it, they have partly failed. If they have a talent and learn somehow to use the whole of it, they have gloriously succeeded, and won a satisfaction and a triumph few persons ever know." –Thomas Wolfe

Chapter 1
Life Is a Special Occasion

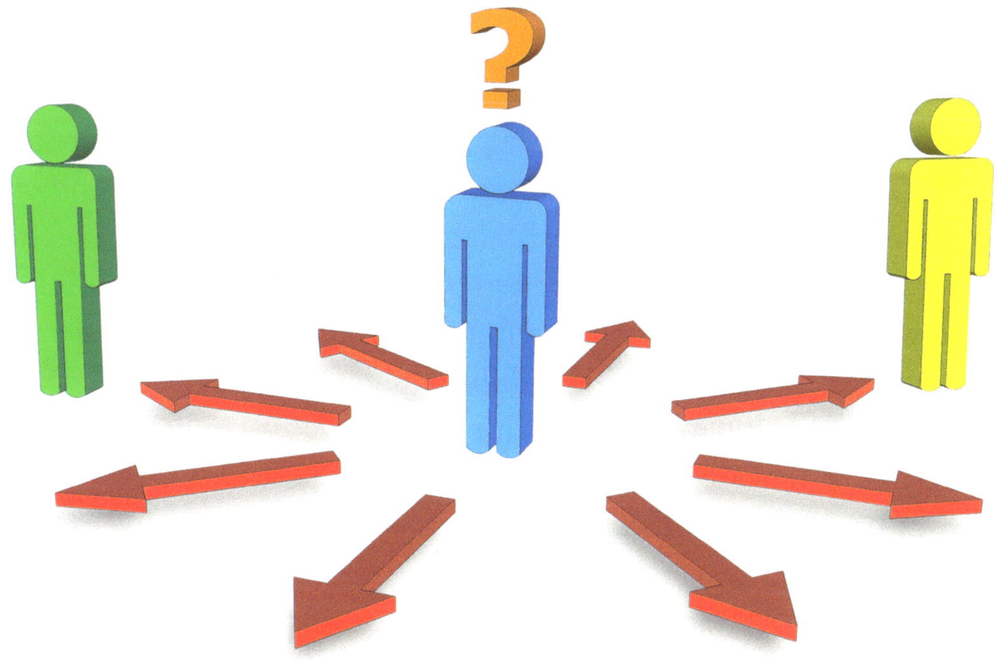

Shutterstock

Have you reached a point in your life where you ask yourself, "Why am I here? What is the point?" At this stage, you begin searching for who you are and trying to determine your destiny—what it is that you are meant to do. Destiny can be defined as the sum of everything that happens to you during your lifetime, the end result or the collective impact of the sum of your experiences. While fate may place opportunities in your path, it is up to you to determine your destiny by your sum life choices.

CRE8IVES tend to wait to be invited into a career by industry gatekeepers. But actually, your followers are waiting for you to invite them into something that moves them. Calls them. Changes them. **DON'T WAIT FOR PERMISSION . . .** You have the ability right now to create something life changing.

What you desire your ultimate destiny to be should be driven by your purpose, and it is your purpose that drives your actions. Your destiny is your long-term direction, while your purpose gives you an "in the here and now" focus to direct your daily actions. While your ultimate destiny draws you to fulfill it, your purpose is the expression of your work toward fulfilling that destiny. Your purpose may change and evolve throughout your lifetime, while your destiny will remain constant. To start achieving that feeling of fulfillment, you must identify your purpose. What are you called to do right now? This is the stepping-stone toward your destiny.

One and all, be aware of how little time we get to spend on this earth. Using age as the reason you can't pursue your dream life is wasting that precious time. While others' aspirations may wilt and fade, those who commit to their dream and work hard can transform their life goals into lifelong passions.

There is nobody like you. Do not compare yourself to others. Each of us have our own separate struggles and purpose to fulfill. Focus on yourself and what you are here to accomplish.

My lifecycle has taught me the value of knowing my sense of right and wrong. Many people have no idea what their values are. Some have simply inherited a scattering of religious tenets from their parents. Others adhere to some unconscious moral code they've gleaned from their peer group. In general, though, if you don't know what you value, your ability to pursue a meaningful life will be inhibited.

I am a Vietnam War combat veteran. Prior to my military enlistment, I was a hippie surfer, living a Rock 'n Roll, let's party lifestyle. What I personally experienced and witnessed in my tour of duty in Southeast Asia was hell on earth. It forever changed my life. Upon my honorable discharge from the Air Force, I gave my life to God and country. If you asked me from that time forward what my values are, my short and sweet answer would simply be God and country.

Values are the framework in which you live your life and help you figure out what's important and what's not. Without a system of values to give your life meaning and to connect you to something bigger than yourself, you'll feel lost and, ultimately, unhappy.

No matter where you are in life, above all, be yourself. Your values system is extremely personal—don't let anyone else dictate it. And once you choose it, live by it. Do so, and each choice you make will be a deeply satisfying and meaningful one.

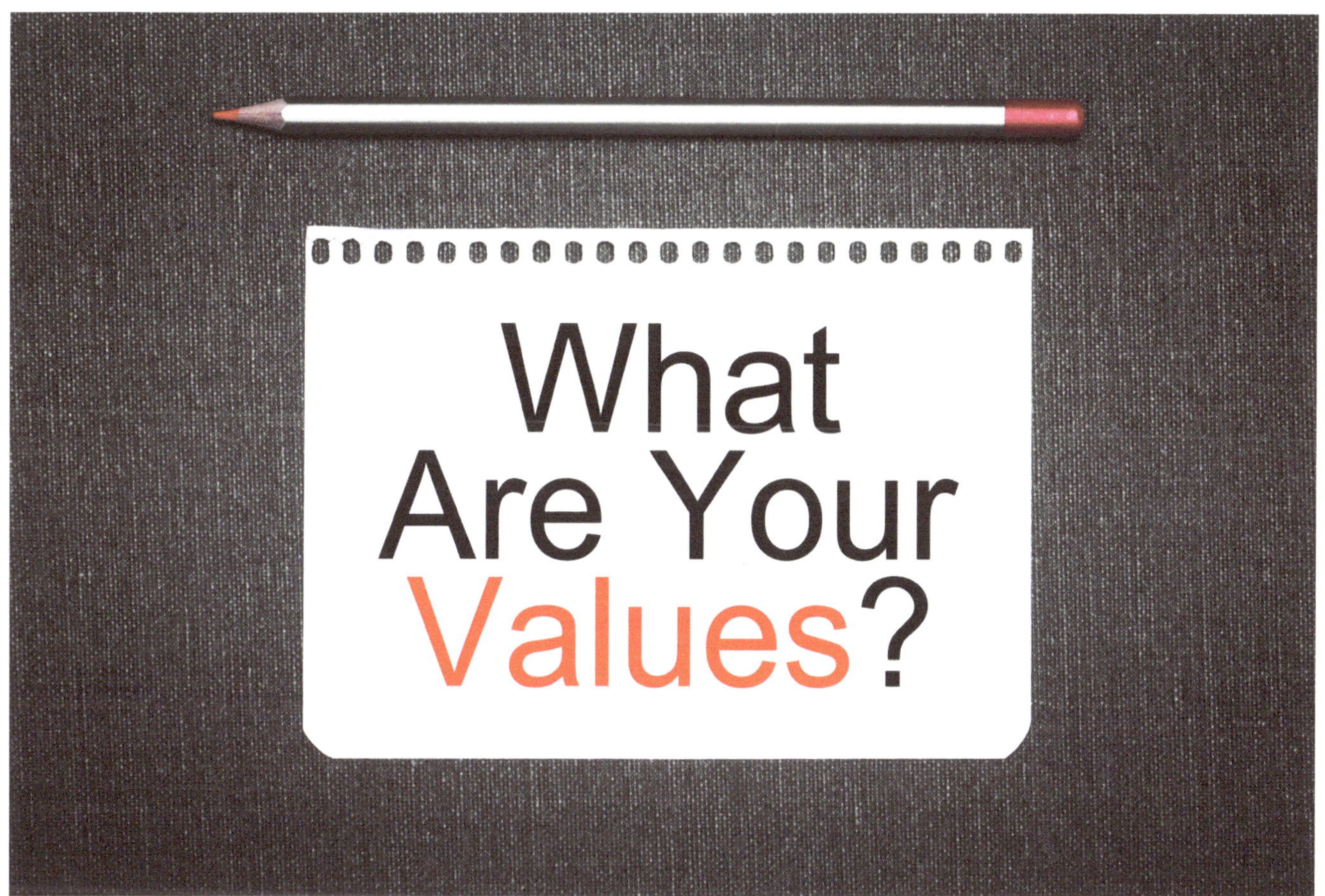

Shutterstock

Briefly State Your Life Values

Values can give goals meaning. It's important to ask yourself, "How does this fit into the bigger picture in my life, and why am I doing this? Is it really a goal that's based on a value I have? Is it something I feel I should or must do?" Ensuring that your goals are in line with who you are—and, especially, who you want to be—makes it much easier to stay on course and committed to these goals and to ultimately achieve them. Your goals can be achieved if you are smart about how you set them and push yourself to get them done, regardless of any outside circumstances. Goals that are tied to who you are, when achieved, will make you feel like a more complete person.

It's critical to enjoy the journey toward your life goals because the journey is life itself. This very moment that is happening right now is when you get to truly experience life itself in all of its beauty, power, and glory.

Achieving goals with straightforwardness is an art many people have yet to master. If you haven't already decided what kind of life you actually want, based on your values, now is the time to do it. Then say no to anything that isn't that. No matter how young or old you are, the stars are still within your reach. You've proven you're smart. What are you going to do with your smarts?

Believe in Yourself
Align Your Life Goals with Your Values

The big understandable, intimidating, looming question is what you should do with your life. What do you really want? You have to go looking for it, and yet what you are looking for is inside you. I have faith that every single person has something special within them. Either they are born with it, or they develop it. Discover your strengths. To excel in your chosen field and to find lasting satisfaction in doing so, you will need to understand your unique strengths.

Your Life's Profession Should Be Derived from Your Deepest Passions

- Passion is the willingness to suffer for something you love.

- What's the one activity that you can't imagine living without   doing?

- Do you believe you cannot succeed unless you are willing to   suffer   for what you love?

- List five things that you love so much it hurts. Rank them in order of how passionate you are about them.

____

____

____

____

____

____

____

Identify Your Dominant Gifts
Talents, Knowledge, and Skills

____

____

____

____

____

____

____

____

Your exceptional talents can grow throughout your life, through good and bad happenstances. Most everyone wants to love what they do and do what they love. If you don't chase your dream, someone will hire you to build theirs.

As you pursue your dream life, the journey will be filled with obstacles and the unpredictable. You'll often be tempted to turn back. Remember that today isn't a rehearsal. This is your life. Everyone has a destiny. If you need a little inspiration or guidance to find your life's purpose, read these quotes to help point you in the right direction.

Diana Ross "You can't just sit there and wait for people to give you that golden dream, you've got to get out there and make it happen for yourself."

Marcus Buckingham "You can find energizing moments in each aspect of your life, but to do so you must learn how to catch them . . . and allow yourself to follow where they lead."

Bishop T. D. Jakes "If you can't figure out your purpose, figure out your passion. For your passion will lead you right into your purpose."

Oprah "There is no greater gift you can give or receive than to honor your calling. It's why you were born. And how you become most truly alive."

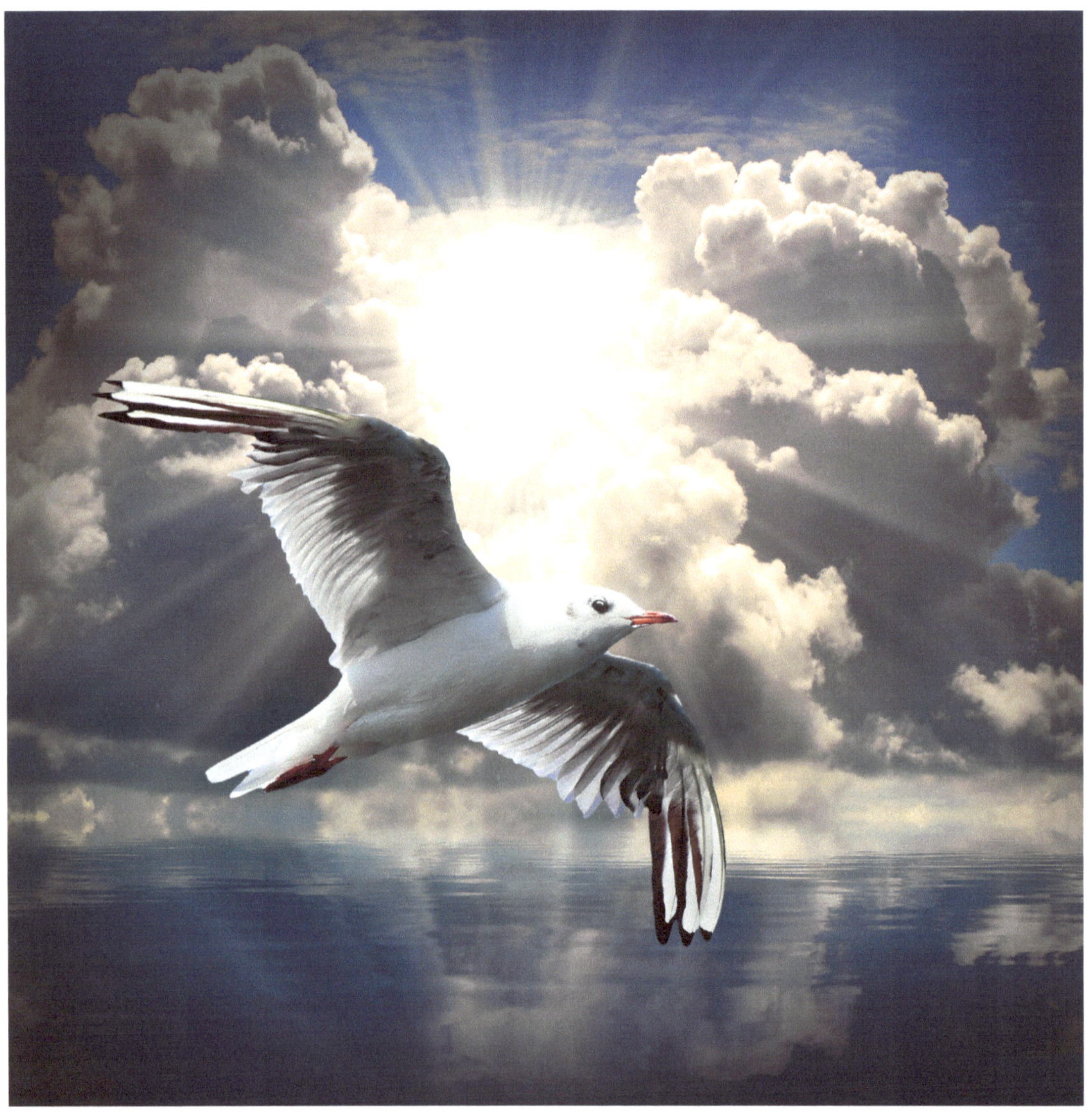

Shutterstock

You can never cross the ocean until you have the courage to lose sight of the shore. Five Steps to Creating Your Future

Step 1: Commit to creating your future.

Step 2: Create a vision of your future.

Step 3: Construct a plan to fulfill your vision.

Step 4: Carry out your plan.

Step 5: Celebrate what you've done—and continue creating your future.

Composing a Statement

A personal vision statement is a key point. It should be short and sweet for a quick response when asked.

- Why have you chosen your creative discipline?

- What is the role of color, motion, sound, light, design in your work?

- Is there anything unusual about the way you employ it?

- Does emotional, social, or political content play a part in your creative work/expression?

- What does your artistic expression say about your ideals?

- How do you feel when creating?

- How do you want others to respond?

- What are the key themes and issues of your work?

- Is there something that people don't understand about your work that you want to address?

Tips

- Those who are not artists or creatives will be reading this, so don't use terminology and cliches.

- Avoid the words *really*, *very*, *however*, and so forth.

- Be direct and concise.

- Keep it simple, no lyrical trips of castles in the sky.

Sample Statement

Chapter 2

Dream Big
Work Hard and Make It Happen

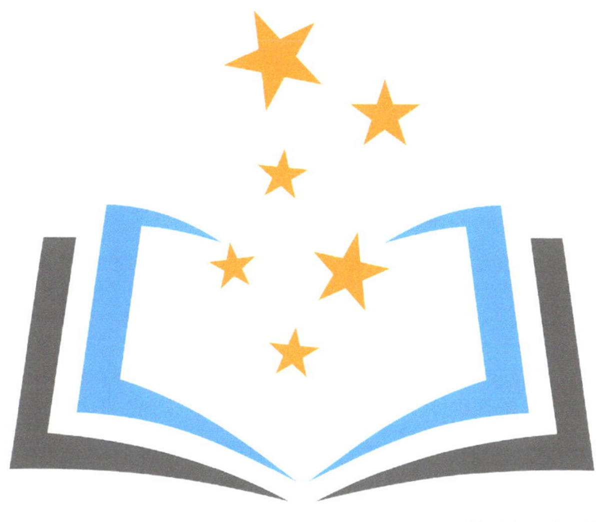

Shutterstock

In Bob Dylan's album *Slow Train Coming*, Dylan performs a song he wrote titled "When You Gonna Wake Up." The lyrics go like this, "You got some big dreams baby, but in order to dream you gotta still be asleep. When you gonna wake up."

Dreams have a long history, both as a subject of conjecture and as a source of inspiration. Throughout their history, people have sought meaning in dreams. They have been described physiologically as a response to neural processes during sleep, psychologically as reflections of the subconscious, and spiritually as messages from God or predictions of the future. Many humans hold different views on the purpose of dreams. Some believe dreams serve no purpose at all, while others believe they can help humans understand their subconscious thought processes to overcome psychological difficulties. In the late 1800s, Sigmund Freud theorized that dreams reflected human desires and were prompted by external stimuli.

A daydream is a fantasy that a person has while awake, often about spontaneous and fanciful thoughts not connected to the person's immediate situation. There are so many different types of daydreaming that there is still no consensus among psychologists about how to define them. While daydreams may include fantasies about future scenarios or plans, reminiscences about past experiences, or vivid dream-like images, they are often connected with some type of emotion.

Wikipedia, the free encyclopedia states that:

> **Imagination** is the power and **process** of producing **mental images** and **ideas**. The term is technically used in **psychology** for the process of reviving in the **mind percepts** of objects formerly given in sense perception. Since this use of the term conflicts with that of ordinary **language**, some psychologists have preferred to describe this process as "**imaging**" or "imagery" or to speak of it as "reproductive" as opposed to "productive" or "constructive" imagination. Imagined images are seen with the "**mind's eye**." A certain unreality is characteristic of imagination, it has great practical importance as a purely ideational activity. Its very freedom from objective limitation makes it a source of pleasure and pain.

Daydreaming may take the form of a train of thought, leading the daydreamer away from being aware of his or her immediate surroundings and concentrating more and more on these new directions of thought. While daydreaming has long been mocked as a lazy, non-productive pastime, as can be seen in the use of the phrase "pipe dream," daydreaming can be constructive in some contexts. There are numerous examples of people in creative or artistic careers, such as composers, novelists, artists, filmmakers, architects, fashion designers, choreographers, and entrepreneurs developing new ideas through daydreaming. Similarly, research scientists, mathematicians, and physicists have developed new ideas by daydreaming about their subject areas. Dr. Martin Luther King Jr. proclaimed he had a dream and went on to change the social culture of America.

In the context of ***CRE8IVES: BE A DREAM ACHIEVER WORKBOOK***, I'm referring primarily to *daydreams as dreams.* We all have dreams—the desire to achieve, the determination to follow through a process, and the drive needed to maintain consistent efforts to accomplish desires and deliver on them, the result of reaching your goals for success. *So, dream—but don't sleep!*

Many times, over the course of my long life, I have shared with family and friends my excitement about a life dream, and more times than not, I've heard the response, *"IT CAN'T BE DONE."*

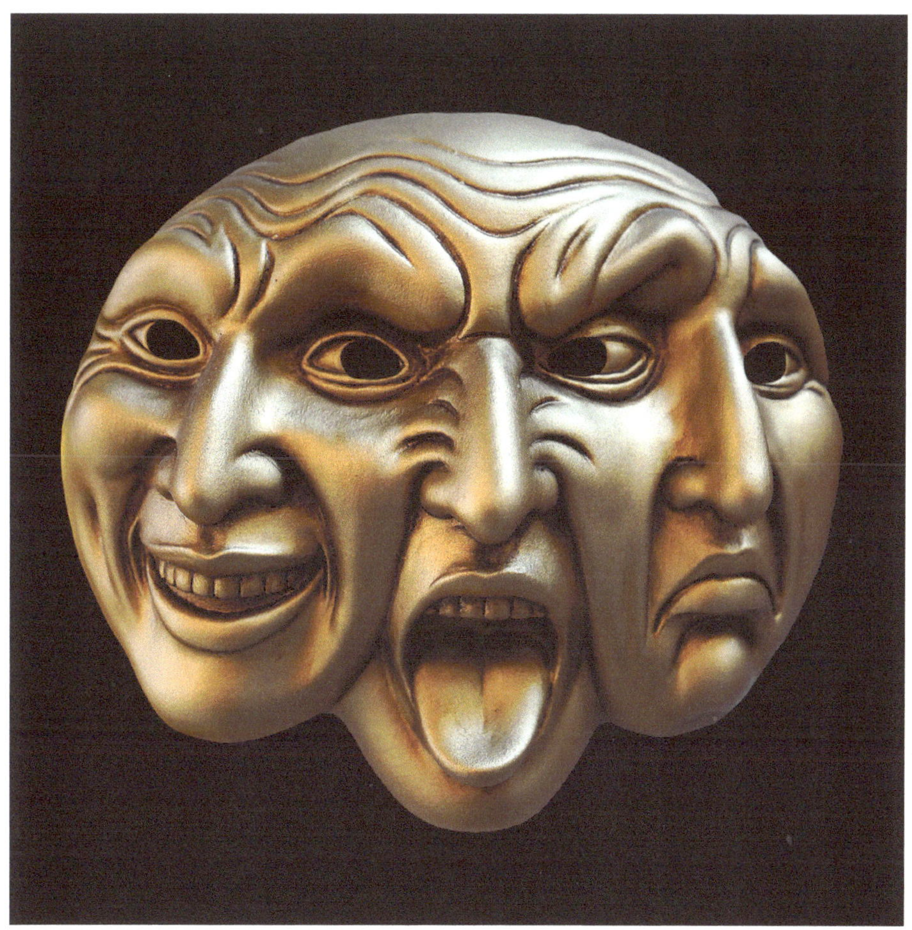

Shutterstock

No one knows your get-up-and-go better than you do. I've learned often when people tell you, "It can't be done," they are putting into words their own uncertainties and lack of self-confidence. Don't let them put an end to your life dream.

Chapter 3
Life Is Now

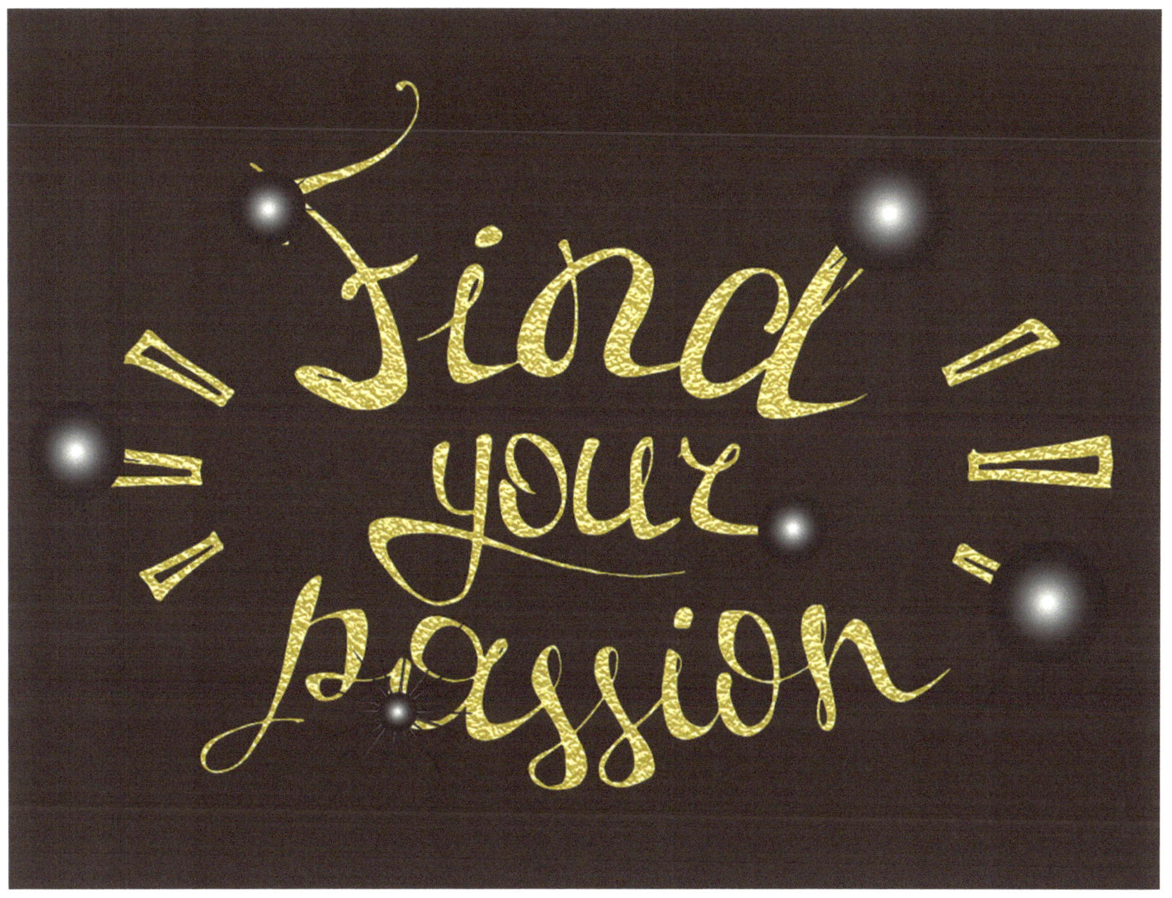

Shutterstock

"End the delusion of time. Time and mind are inseparable. Remove time from the mind and it stops—unless you choose to use it. The eternal present is the space within which your whole life unfolds. The one factor that remains constant. LIFE IS NOW. There was never a time when your life was not NOW, nor will there ever, ever be. Nothing ever happened in the past. It happened in the NOW. Nothing will ever happen in the future; it will happen in the NOW."

—Eckhart Tolle

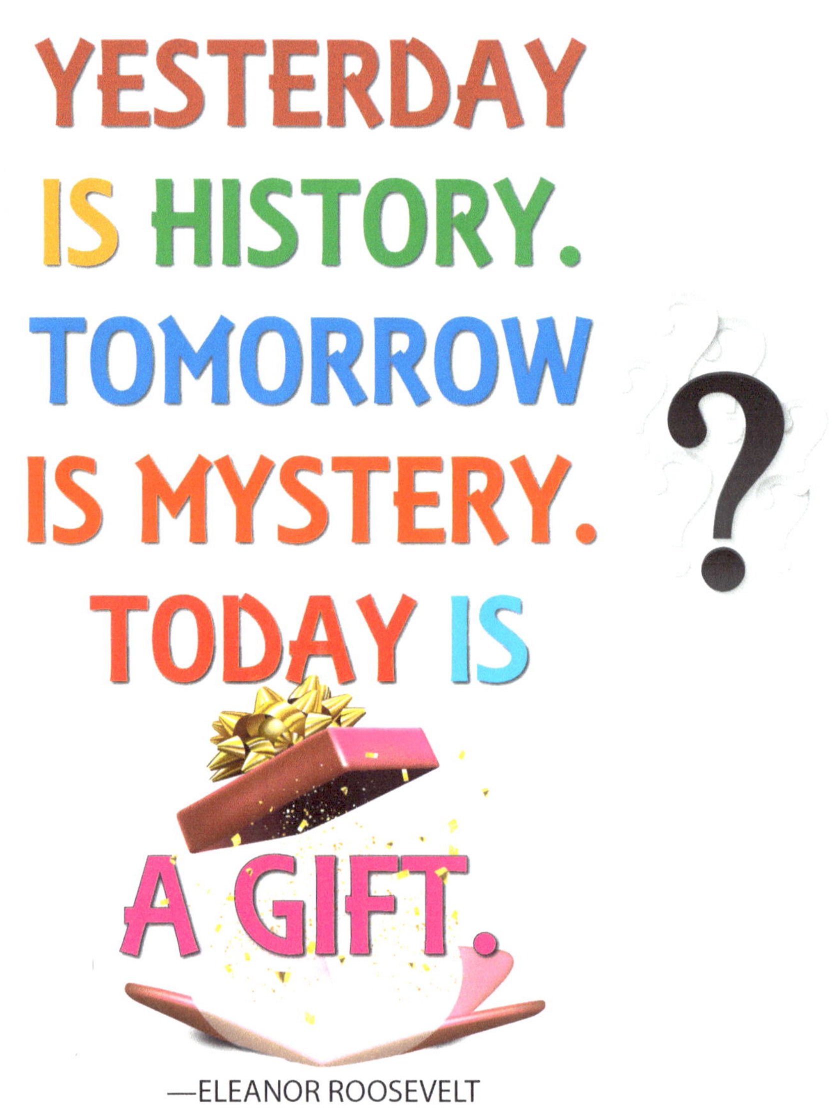

Nancy McKarney

Living Out Your Dream Career in the Here and Now
The ABCs of Career Development

MOTIVATIONAL MYTHS

You can *be* whatever you want to be is a lie. Not everyone can be whatever he or she wants to be. Not everyone can be a fine artist or an actor or a musician or a dancer or a movie star, to name a few of the CRE8IVES. You can become whatever you have the potential to become and are willing to dedicate the time and effort into becoming, and what you have the talent for.

You can *do* whatever you want to do. Wrong. Much like the preceding myth, it will only lead to disappointment. You can do whatever you have the talent to do. And you have more talent to do more things than you have given yourself credit for up until now.

You can *have* whatever you want to have. The truth is, you can have whatever you believe you deserve, and whatever you take action toward achieving, utilizing your abilities, your thoughts, and your words. The real issue with these three myths is the word **want**. You do not get what you want; you get what you take action on.

HAVE THE COURAGE TO DREAM

Who are you?

What is your dream idea?

Why?

Where will it be?

When?

How?

A CRE8IVES'S LIFE IS FILLED WITH DREAMS

Melody for a song
A poem
Your next painting, sculpture
Theatrical performance
Book to write
Film to produce
A new fashion design
Your next entrepreneurial development

"The greatest danger for most of us lies not in setting our aim too high and falling short; but in setting our aim too low and achieving our mark." —Michelangelo

IT'S DEMEANING THAT ALL TOO OFTEN DREAMS ARE THOUGHT OF AS OUTRAGEOUS EXPECTATIONS. DREAMS DO NOT HAVE TO BE UNREAL.

Dreams are the mental pictures that inspire virtually every real human endeavor, from the ancient Egyptians dreams of building the Great Pyramids to your dream of a successful career in the arts. Dreams contain nearly limitless power to lift us up in a world that sometimes seems determined to hold us down. Dreams have the power to pull us forward in the face of adversity. Dreams have the power to sharpen our focus and fill our lives with energy and passion. Dreams have the power to renew our strength and shield us from criticism and negative thinking.

The Mystery of Breakthrough Creativity

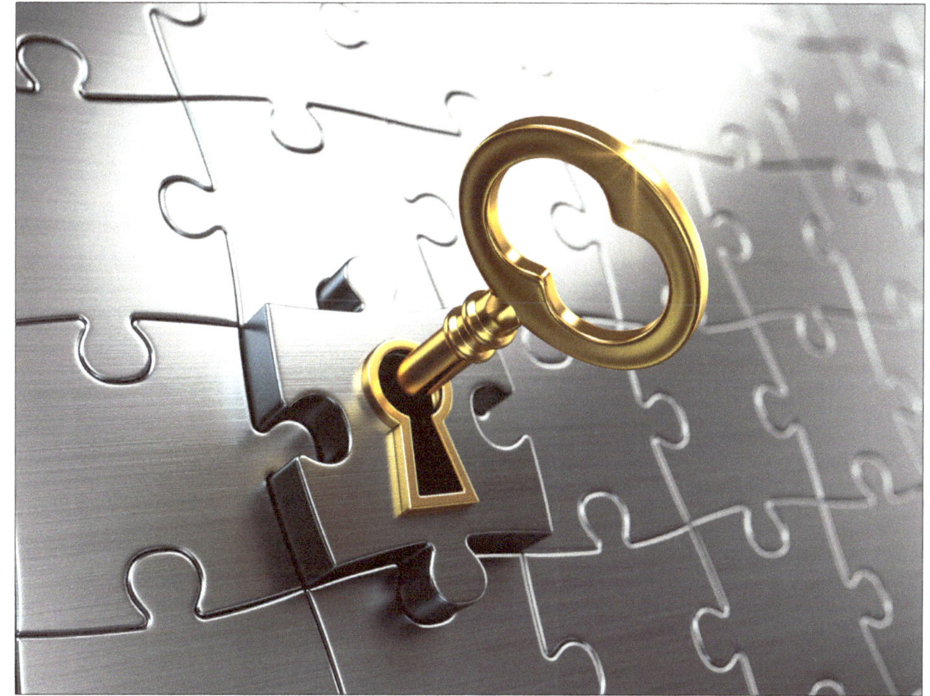

Shutterstock

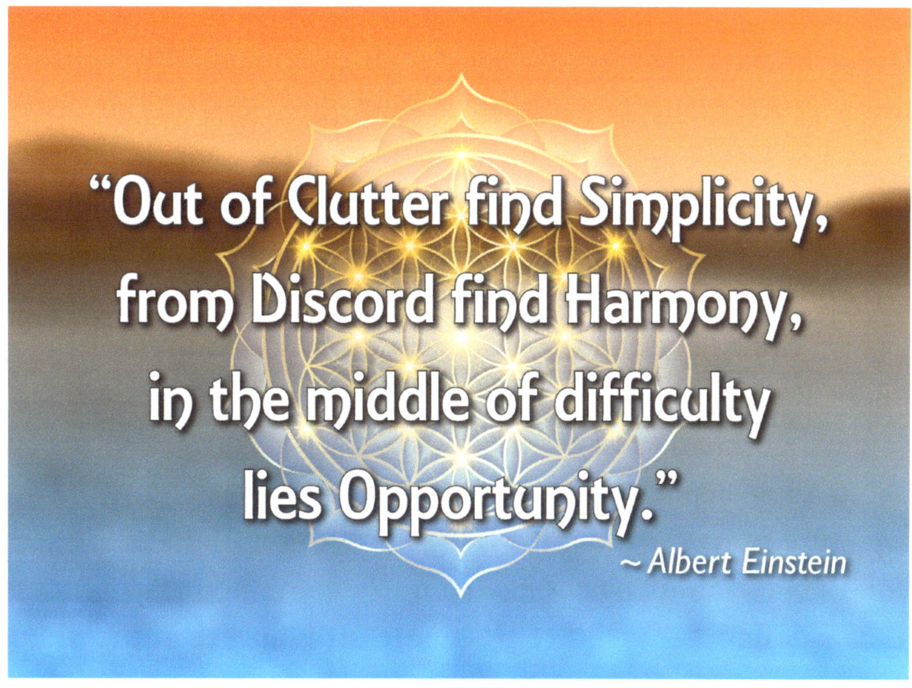

Nancy McKarney

The sudden flash of inspiration.
The surprising emergence of a
Meaningful pattern in the midst of complexity.
The discerning reframing of a problem.
The leap to a whole new space of ideas.

IMAGINATION

INTUITION

INSIGHT

EQUALS

CREATIVITY

I have learned much about America's innovative thinkers and entrepreneurial trailblazers from studying the work of journalist and author Harold Evan. His book, *They Made America* and the PBS television series by the same name explores the political, social, economic, and environmental forces that have made the United States an incubator for so many radical and far-reaching creative entrepreneurs. One of the chronicles that has astonished me is how Ruth Marianna Handler, an American businesswoman, created the Barbie doll. Ruth was born Ruth Marianna Mosko in Denver, Colorado, to Polish-Jewish immigrants Ida and Jacob Mosko. She married her high school boyfriend, Elliot Handler, and moved to Los Angeles in 1938. Her husband decided to make their furniture out of two newfound types of plastics, Lucite and Plexiglas. Ruth suggested that he start doing this commercially, and they began a furniture business. Ruth worked as the sales force for the new business, landing contracts with Douglas Aircraft Company and others.

Elliot Handler and his business partner Harold "Matt" Matson formed a small company to manufacture picture frames, calling it "Mattel" by combining part of their names (Matt and Elliot). Later, they began using scraps from the manufacturing process to make doll-house furniture. The dollhouse furniture was more profitable than the picture frames, and it was decided to concentrate on toy manufacturing. The company's first big-seller was the "Uke-a-doodle," a toy ukulele. Ruth served as the vice president, and her husband Elliot was president of the toy manufacturer Mattel Inc.

The Handler's daughter Barbara, who was becoming a pre-teen, played with paper dolls by pretending they were adults. Ruth noticed that in such play, Barbara and her girlfriends would act out future events, rather than the present. Ruth noticed the limitations of the paper dolls, including how the paper clothing failed to attach well. The only kind of dolls being produced and readily available in the marketplace were baby dolls. Ruth realized that little girls as they grow older want to be more than mothers. They someday want to be dreamy and exciting. They someday want to have gorgeous clothes and look like movie stars. Ruth realized that many little girls wanted to be more than mothers with babies.

Ruth imagined producing a three-dimensional plastic doll with an adult body and a wardrobe of fabric clothing. However, her husband and Mr. Matson thought parents would not buy their children a doll with a voluptuous figure.

While the Handler family were vacationing in Europe, Ruth saw the West German Bild Lilli doll (which was not a children's toy, but rather an adult gag gift) in a Swiss shop. Ruth bought it and brought it home. The Lilli doll was a representation of the same doll concept Ruth had imagined and had been trying to sell to her husband and Mr. Matson. This doll was different than the baby-like dolls that girls would play with during this time in America. Ruth was inspired. Up until this point in time, there was a lack of dolls for girls who were old enough to comprehend the basic concepts of being a teenager and adulthood. Once home, Ruth reworked the design of the German Bild Lilli doll. Her vision would be an eleven-inch plastic doll, and she would name it after her daughter, Barbara. Barbie was unlike any doll ever created. Many pessimists predicted that her dream child would be a flop. The doll was rejected by the toy world. Sears said a shapely doll would never grace their toy displays.

Barbie's coming-out debut was at the New York Toy Fair on March 9, 1959. Ruth's dream, the true Barbie doll, was not an immediate success. Ruth didn't give up. When Disney introduced *The Mickey Mouse Club* children's television show, Mattel invested heavily in television advertising, introducing Barbie to the young girl viewers. The TV commercials paid off.

Barbie sold for only $3.00. The profit and excitement lay in the clothes and the accessories. Barbie was a shopper, and so were her millions of fans. Barbie generated enthusiasm and excitement with both little girls and adolescents. With Barbie, they could fantasize about being a fashion model or an airline stewardess.

Within a year, Ruth Handler's doll was getting 10,000 fan letters a week. It took Mattel three years to catch up with the demand. Barbie became the most popular toy in history. The Beautiful Barbie Doll rocketed Mattel and the Handlers to fame and fortune. Subsequently, they would add a boyfriend for Barbie named Ken, after the Handler's son, and many other "friends and family" to Barbie's world.

Ruth Handler imagined, envisioned, and designed the Barbie Doll, which has sold over a billion copies worldwide. She was a founder and vice president of the world's largest toy company, which at its peak had 18,000 employees and annual sales of over $300 million. By the mid-1960s, Barbie was on her way to becoming a *global icon*. Barbie dolls are now sold in 150 countries.

TURN YOUR DREAMS INTO DESTINY

STAGE ONE: *Imagine* your dream

STAGE TWO: *Predict* your dream

STAGE THREE: *Design* your dream

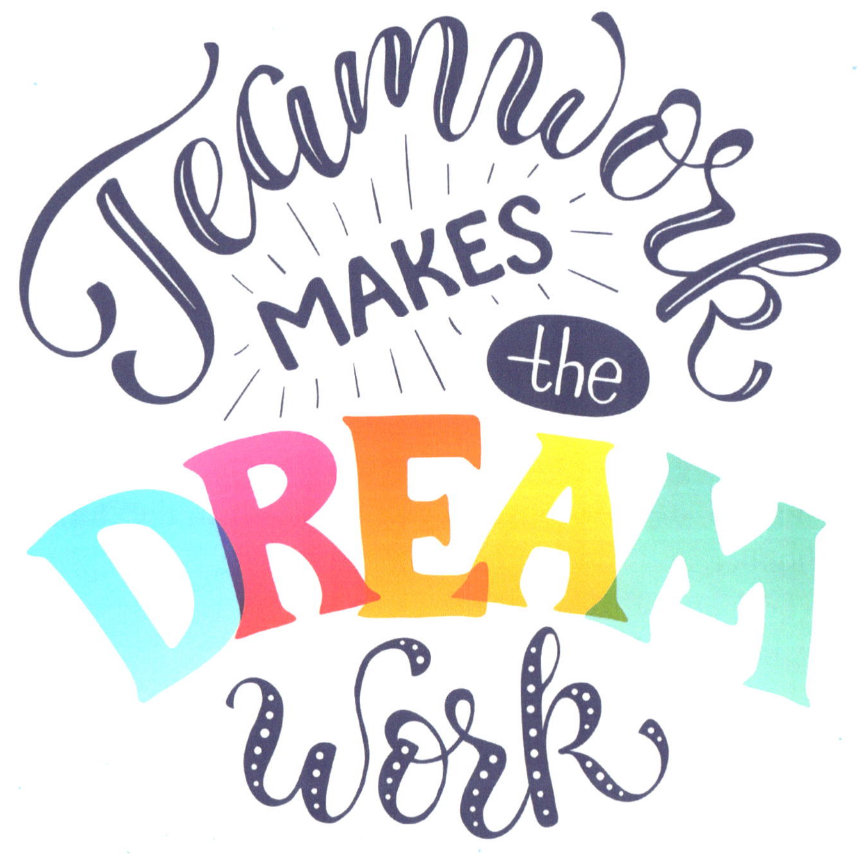

Shutterstock

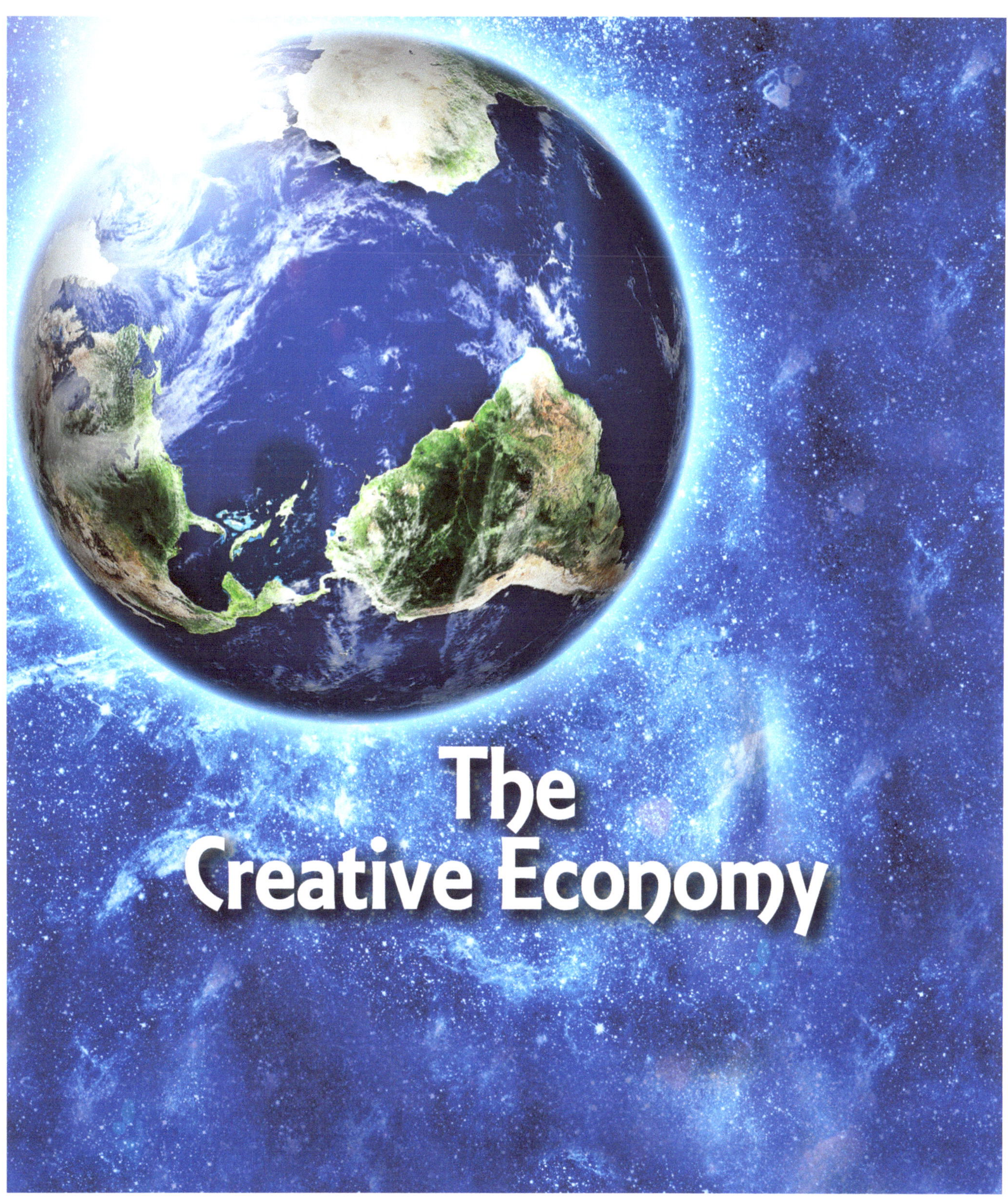

The
Creative Economy

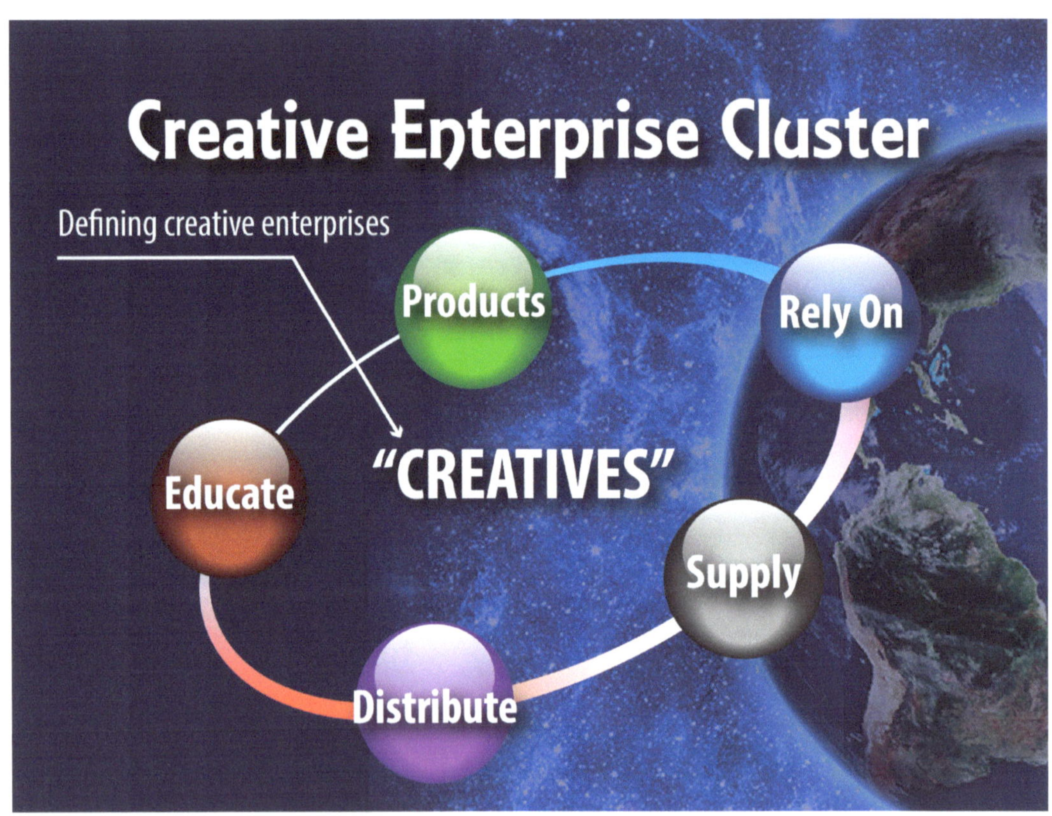

The Creative Economy

- This strategy forces companies to rely more on innovation, image, and aesthetics

- The sectors most likely to grow and create jobs are knowledge–intensive companies that employ highly talented and creative workers

- Companies that depend on art and design and those that produce artistic or designer goods or services

The Creative Economy

• Moreover, consumer demand for authentic and unique goods, many made by small businesses and entrepreneurs, is a growing proportion of many economies, particularly in rural communities.

• The most important aspect of these knowledge –and arts–intensive goods and services companies is that they are much more apt to be produced in higher wage, industrialized countries.

Crafting a New Strategy
The Art of Economic Development

Give Companies New Competitive Advantages

Add To Community and Cultural Resources

Educate and Support Artisans

Attract Non-traditional Learners With Creative Talent

Economic Rationale for Focusing on Creativity and Culture

- Arts and craft based enterprises collectively produce significant wealth
- Firms most likely to continue to produce goods in the U.S. Will be technology–or fashion / design –based
- Creative communities attract talent and good jobs
- Talent exists across geographic, racial, ethnic, and class boundaries

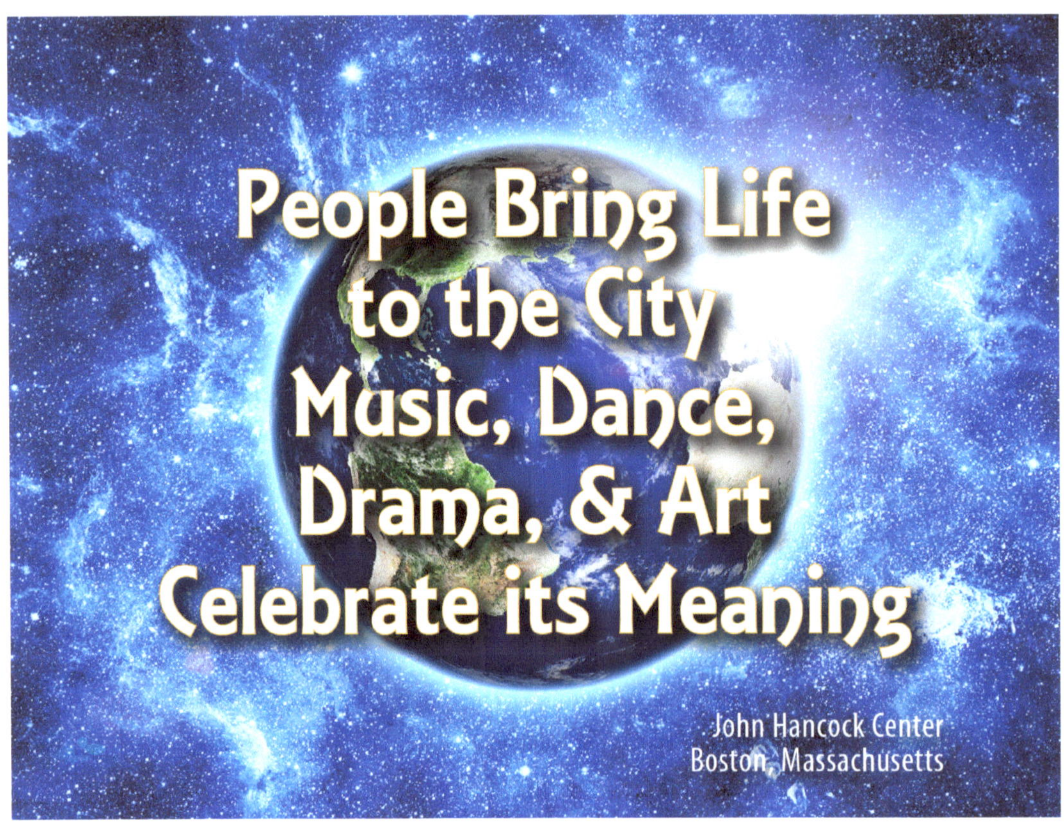

The United States Economy
Free Enterprise

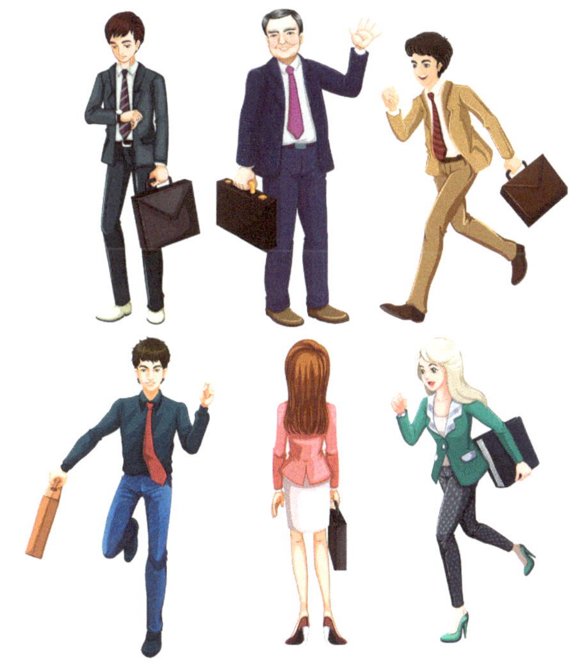

Shutterstock

The Capitalist Engine

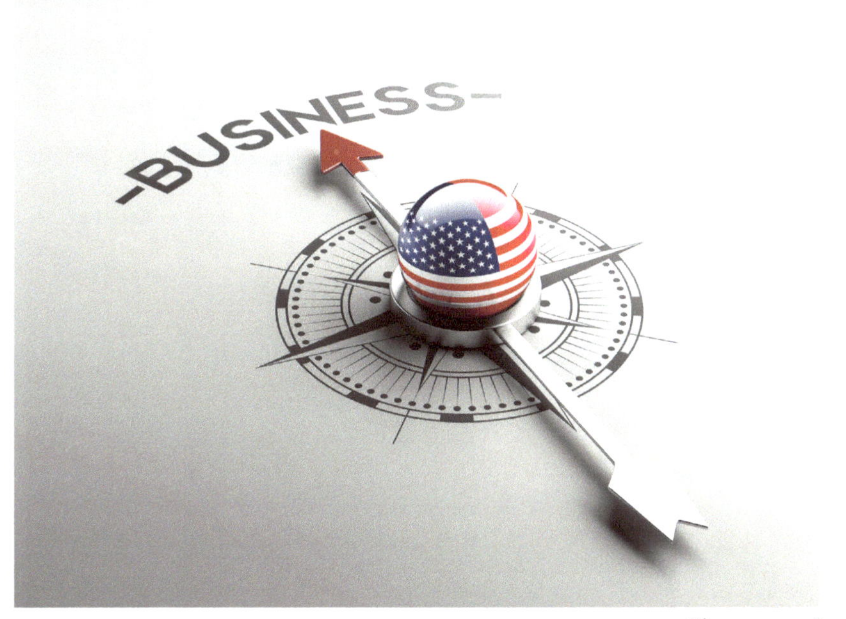

Shutterstock

Free enterprise is usually considered to involve the rights of individuals and groups of individuals acting as "legal persons" or corporations to trade capital goods, labor, land, and money.

Physical Capital

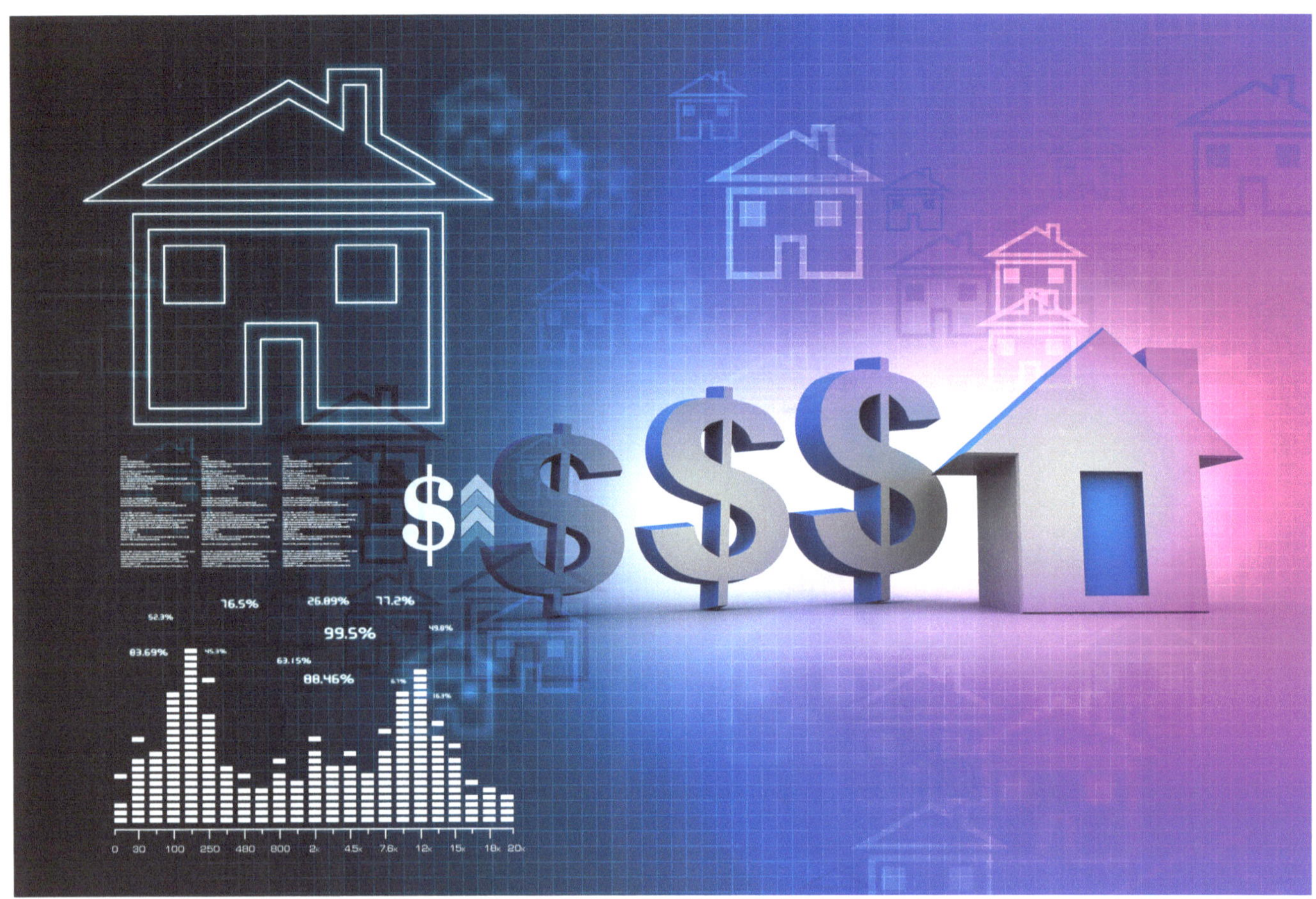

Shutterstock

Human Capital

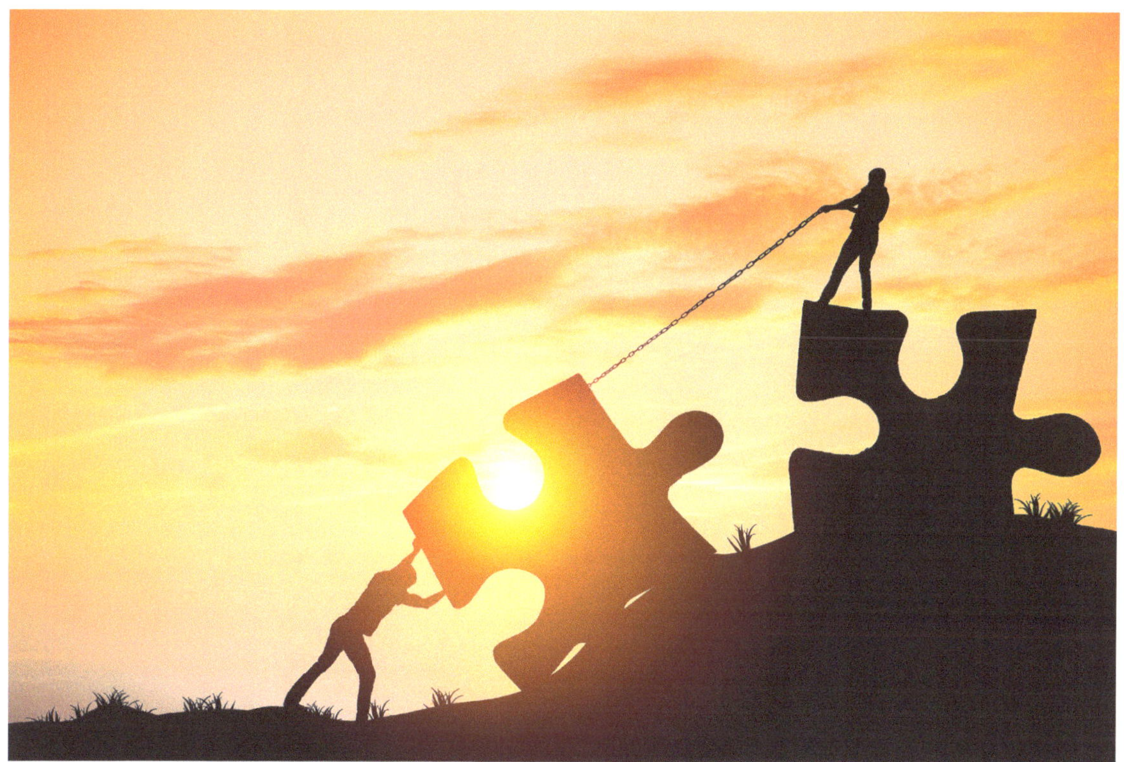

Shutterstock

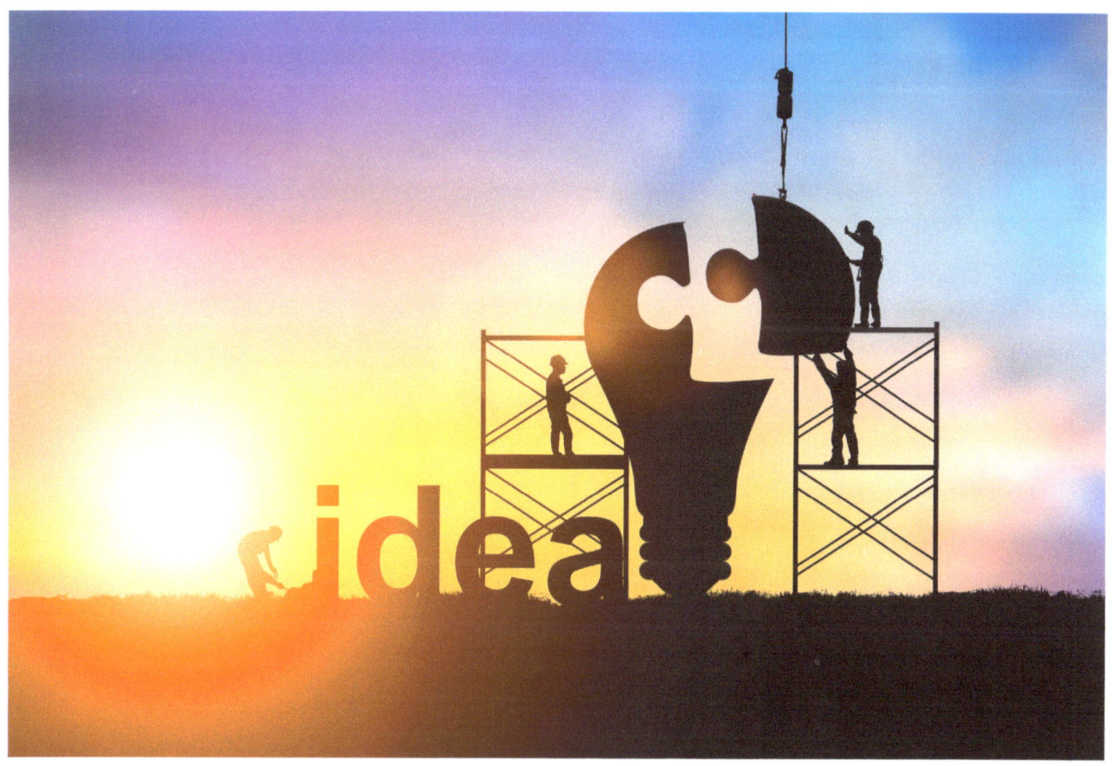

Shutterstock

Intellectual Capital

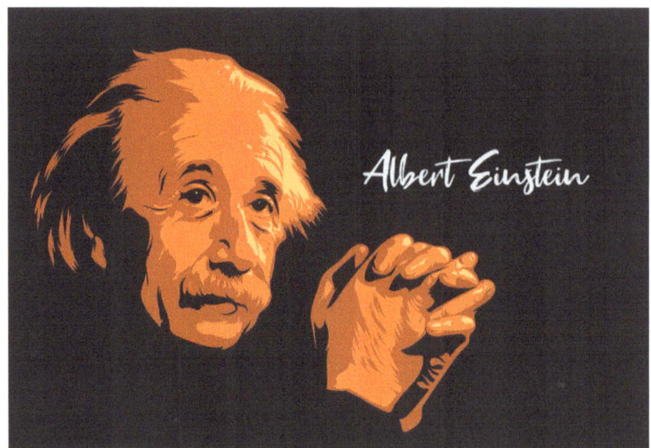

Shutterstock

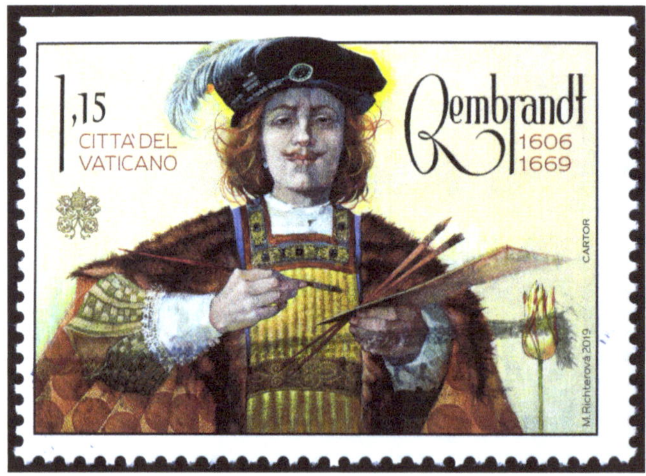

Shutterstock

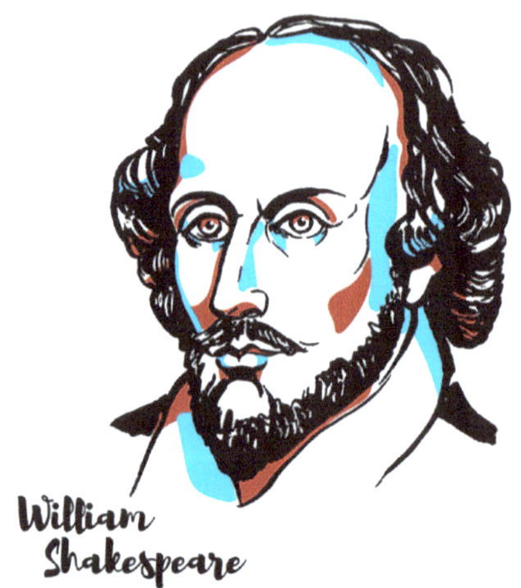

Shutterstock

Economic Development

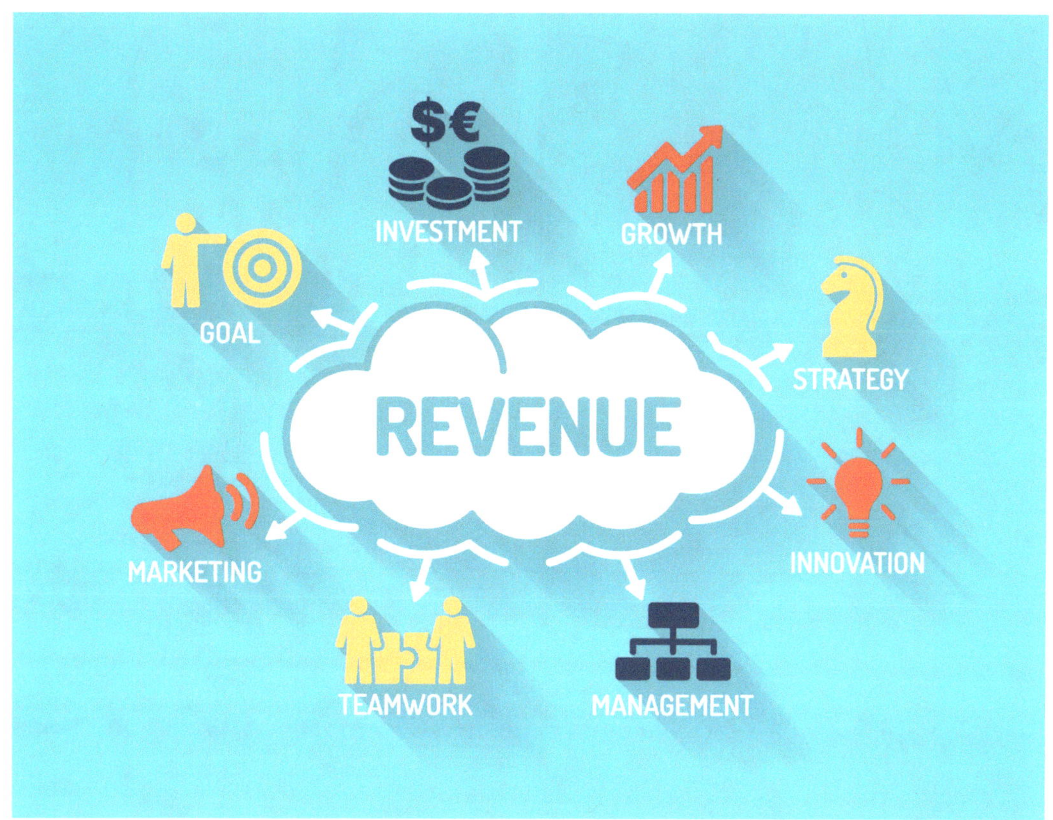

Shutterstock

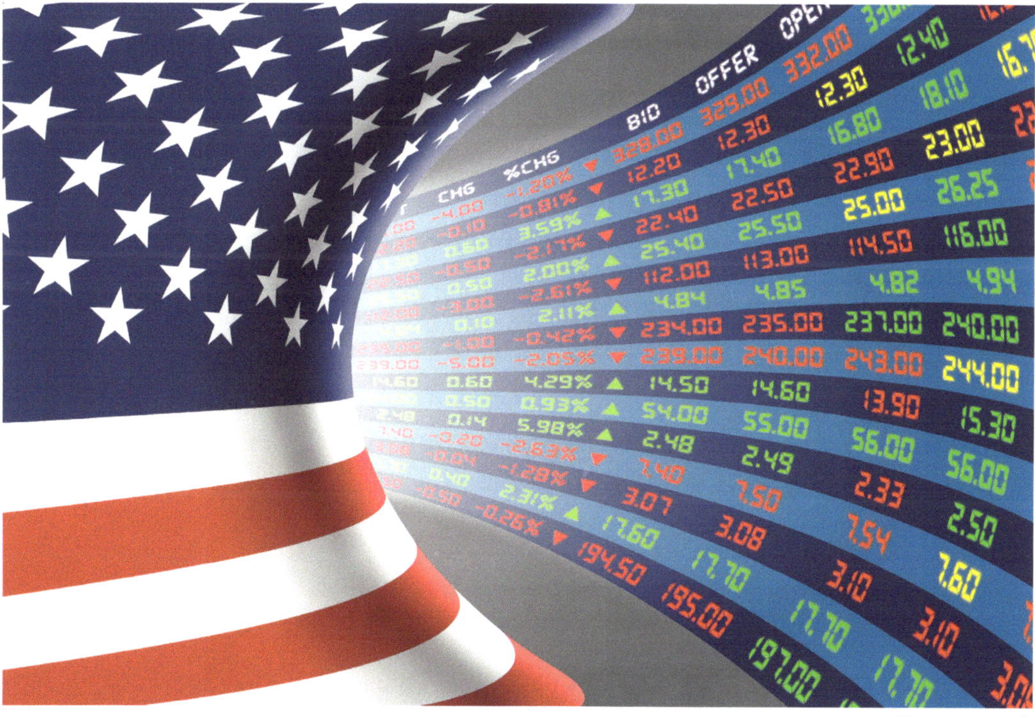

Shutterstock

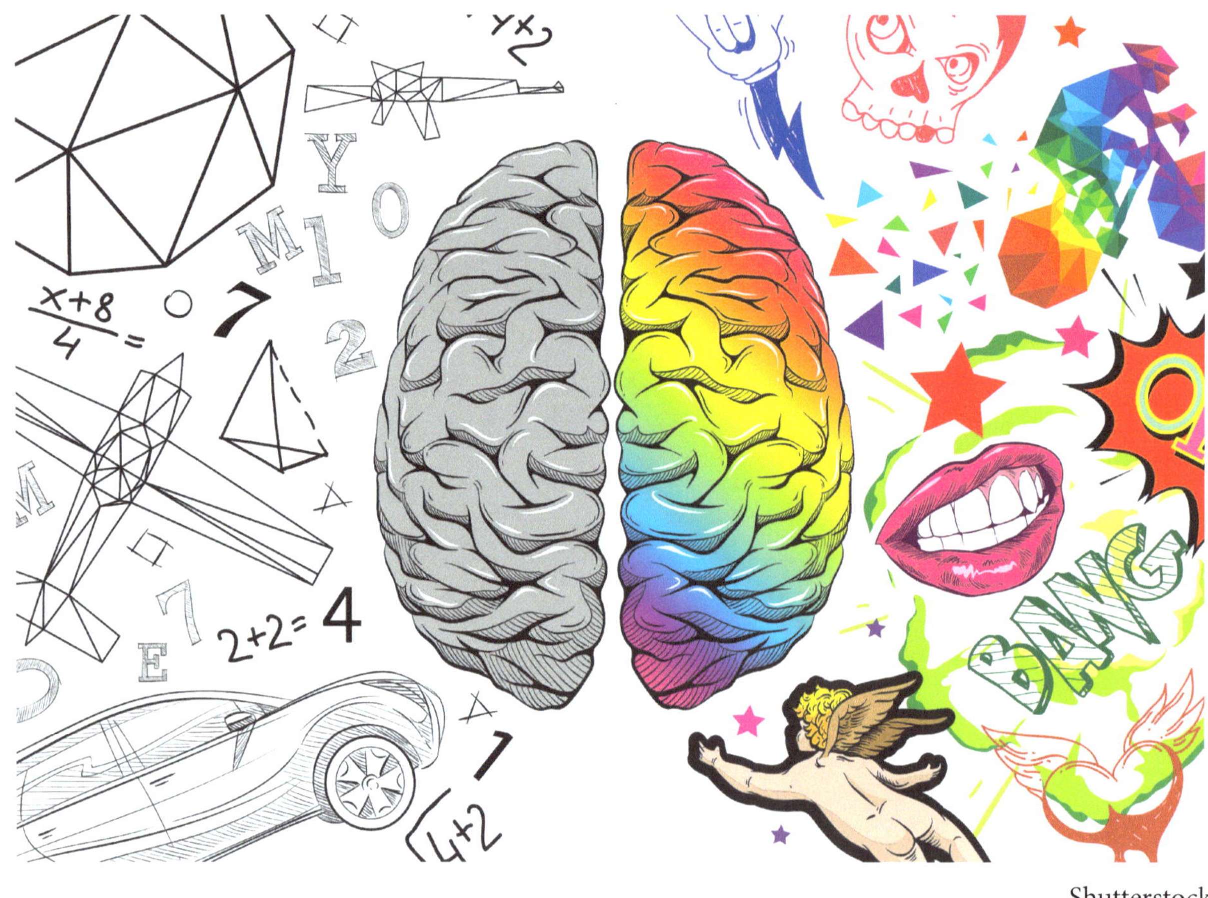

Shutterstock

Paradigms

- ➤ Paradigms are *ideas—spaces*.

- ➤ A paradigm, like a lens, reveals the world to us, but it also conceals.

- ➤ Paradigms conceal in the sense of imposing limits on how far speculative thinking can go.

- ➤ The formation of a new paradigm opens up new ways of seeing and thinking that can overcome the limitations of the old one. Examples are:

Galileo's theory of pendulums
Newtonian mechanics
Dalton's discovery of atomic weights
Einstein's relativity theories

All represent the emergence of new paradigms that revolutionize the course of scientific research.

➢ Creative people deal in future possibilities.

➢ The root meaning of invent is "to find," from Latin *invenire.*

➢ Entrepreneurs dream that somewhere out there, in the realm of possibilities, is a very different world, a new idea-space characterized by its own distinct form of embedded intelligence.

➢ Like Columbus setting sail for what he thought were the Indies, the entrepreneur is often not quite sure what or where this new world is and may even eventually wind up in a different place from the one, he or she is planning.

➢ Gutenberg recognized in cheese and oil presses a mechanism for improving the cumbersome printing process of his day.

➢ After spotting a Holt Caterpillar tractor at work, Ernest Swinton invented the tank, solving the difficulties traditional wheeled vehicles encountered, moving over trenches during World War I.

➢ Velcro was invented by a Swiss engineer who, finding cockleburs clinging to his pants after a walk through the fields, put them under a microscope and saw tiny hooks that acted as remarkably efficient fastening mechanisms.

➢ The sports bra was invented when two entrepreneurial-minded women, horsing around with a couple of male jockstraps, suddenly recognized the basic design and need for a female athletic support.

The drive for creative breakthrough is one of the central dynamic forces of the Western world, the means whereby it has transformed itself into the most complex, powerful, wealthy, culturally enriched, and scientifically and technologically advanced society in history. Breakthrough creativity has been in the historian Joel Mokyr's trenchant phrase,
"The West's Lever of Riches."

dream
BIG

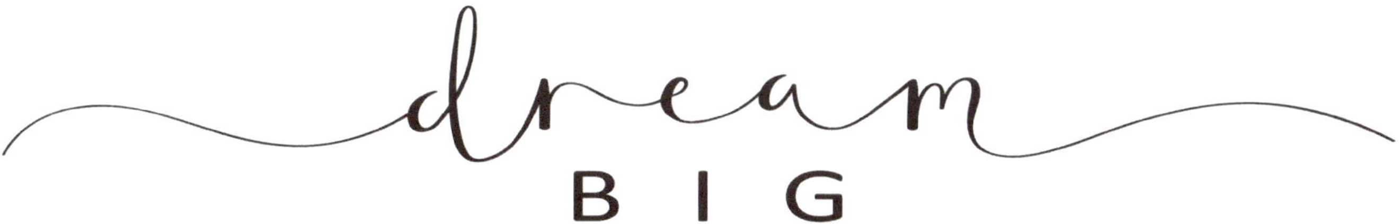

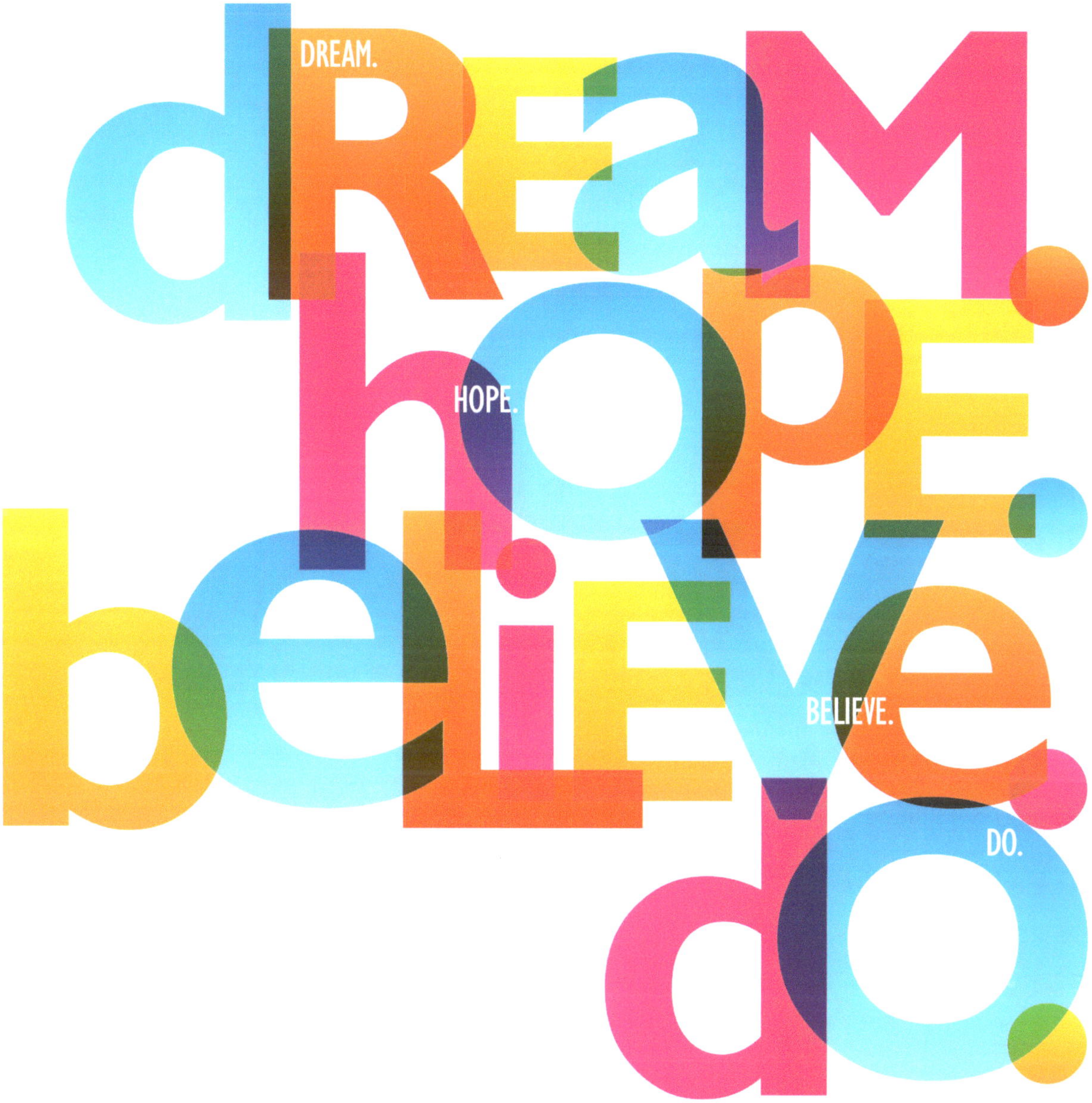

Count The Costs

- o The **DREAM** is not for **FREE**

- o You are going to pay a price to realize the **DREAM**

- o **FEAR** can be a bad enemy

- o **FEAR** can cause you to make bad decisions

    - ➢ **F** alse

    - ➢ **E** vidence

    - ➢ **A** appearing

    - ➢ **R** eal

Make It Happen

- o Be Solution-Oriented

- o Be Willing To Develop New Talents

- o Make Achievement a Core Personal Value

- o Remain Patient

Chapter 5

Every Day Is a New Beginning

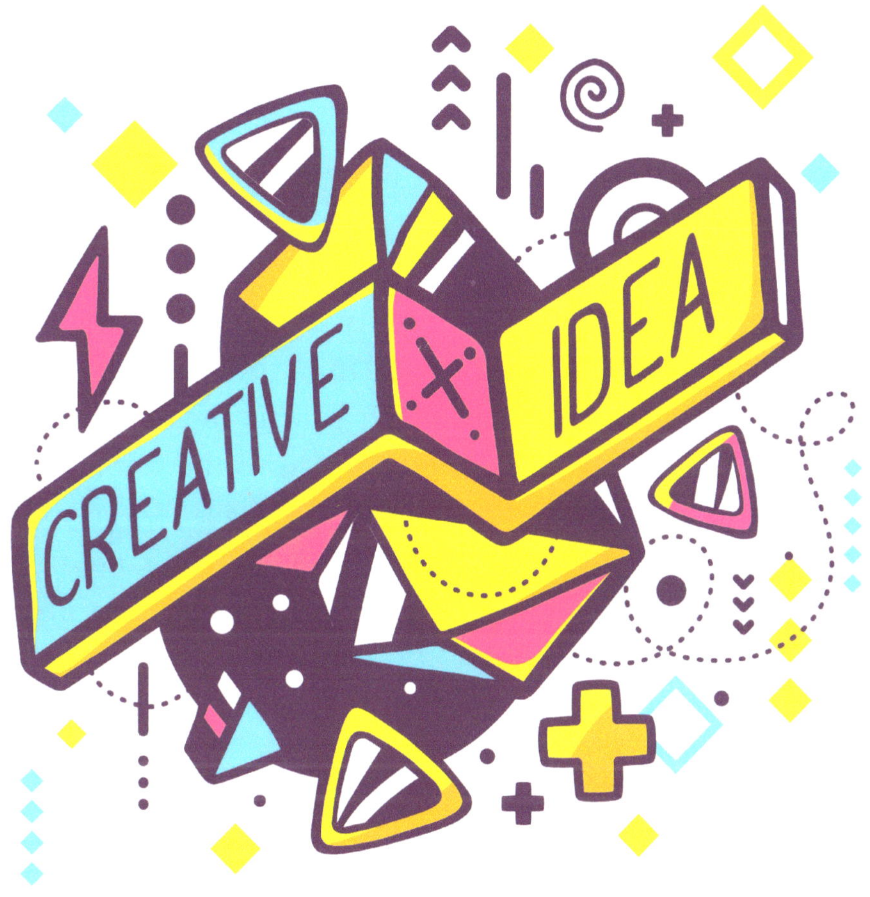

Shutterstock

Everyone has their own unique purpose and path to walk in this world, so try to stay focused. Don't worry too much about what other people are working on or whether they seem to be making more progress than you. You are doing things in your own time and in your own way, and that's exactly how it's supposed to be.

The awful truth about planning is that plans are pure fiction. There never was a plan that happened the way it was written. At the same time, planning is a smart thing to do because it gets you into action. Action provides you with many happy accidents. While you're calling people, looking things up online, even if you find yourself in one blind alley after another, you're sure to stumble on unexpected opportunities. The very unpredictability of life turns into an asset because you don't have to have all the answers, just the general direction and a willingness to show up. **Woody Allen said, "Eighty percent of success is showing up."**

When you start planning steps on paper, wishful thinking does an about-face and becomes a to-do list, just as real as a grocery list. A plan gets you out of your head and into the world, where reality will provide the pieces to your puzzle. This is the pivotal point of a real transformation. When dreams don't make it to the planning stage, they stay in the clouds, never to become reality. When plans push you into action, however, all kinds of benefits flood into your life. Alone with your dreams, you think you have to create everything on your own, but out in the world, you find much will come to meet you.

THE PAST IS YOUR LESSON. THE PRESENT IS YOUR GIFT. THE FUTURE IS YOUR MOTIVATION.

Three key reasons why it's so critical to start with the end in view:

1. It gets you started right.

"All's well that ends well."

"All's well that begins well."

Determine where you want to go.

Identify your passions and your gifts.

Identify someone who has been successful in the areas that interests you, a role model.

Watch how they live. Listen to them. Absorb all you can from them. Then use what you've learned to help pinpoint your destination or goal.

2. It keeps you going.

When you start with the end in view, you don't waste your energy shooting at unnecessary targets.

Watching your desired "end" get closer can also motivate you to keep going. We all need encouragement as the excitement of starting turns into the sometimes-exhausting business of daily life and work.

3. It gets you where you need to go.

What gets measured gets done!

Abraham Lincoln said, "I will get ready and perhaps my chance will come."

Soren Kierkegaard stated, "Life can only be understood backwards, but it must be lived forwards."

John Wooden, legendary basketball coach asserted, "It's too late to prepare when the opportunity comes."

These three leaders understood the value of getting ready for today with an eye fixed firmly on the future. If you want to increase your chances of success, start with the end in view. ***The journey begins in the mirror!***

CONQUER YOUR DREAM

There is no better time than the present to accomplish your biggest goals. Spend time thinking about your dream and brainstorm some steps you need to take to get there. Clarity is key—when your mind is unwavering and clear about the path you need to be on, you really can accomplish all, no matter what!

Have a daily daydream about your dream—imagine what it looks like, how it makes you feel, and who it brings into your life.

Create a dream board and paste pictures, words, or articles of anything that represents your dream onto it.

Write the story about your dream. Record it and listen to it each night before bedtime.

Tell others about your dream. It's absolutely okay to reach out to others and ask them for advice, hands-on help, or even just moral support. The more that you have the courage to do so, the more you will inspire others around you to do the same. You never know who can help you. As long as you choose the right people to tell by sharing your goals, reaching out for assistance, and asking people for support, you not only learn how to do it more effectively, but you also gain a support team that can help you in achieving your goals.

Most people reserve celebrations for when they've finally reached the finish line of a goal or dream. There's absolutely no reason you can't celebrate each baby step you take along the way. In fact, taking a moment to celebrate your incremental accomplishments is a sure-fire way to boost your spirits and replenish your well of motivation.

Talk about your dream, using positive words as if you believe and expect it will happen. You should believe and expect it will happen!

Imagine how your dream will help others. How will it enable you to give back?

STEP ONE: *Write* a Personal Vision Statement

STEP TWO: *Write* Down Your Goals

STEP THREE: *Write* a To-Do-List

Your Personal Vision Statement

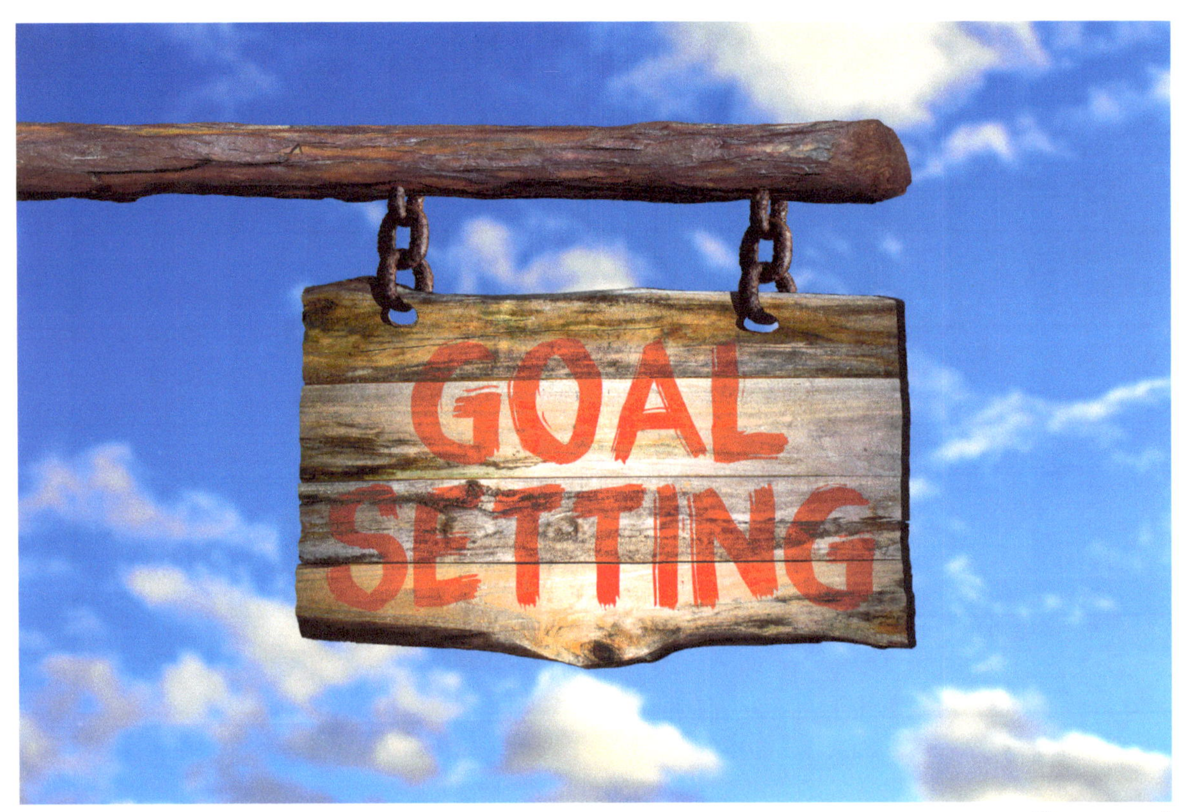

Shutterstock

Your To-Do List

Chapter 6

Dreams

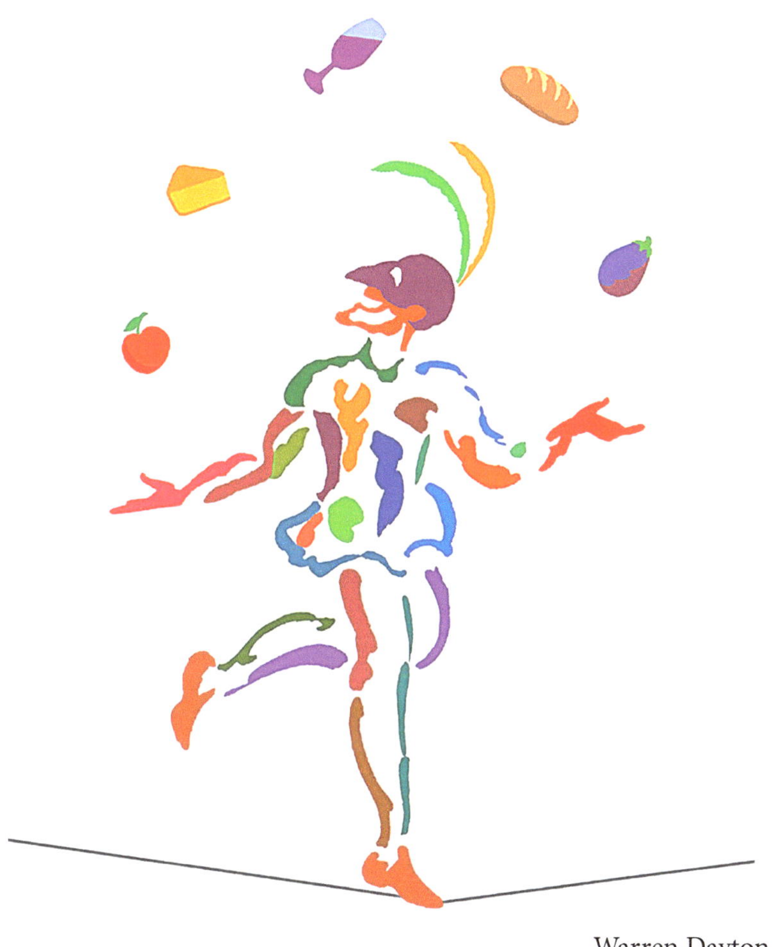

Warren Dayton

Every great dream begins with a dreamer. Always remember, you have within you the strength, the time, and the passion to reach for the stars to change the world.

C. S. Lewis was a British writer. He is best known for his works of fiction, especially *The Screwtape Letters*, *The Chronicles of Narnia*, and *The Space Trilogy*. Lewis wrote more than thirty books, which have been translated into more than thirty languages and have sold millions of copies. Lewis said, "You are *never too old to set another goal or dream a new dream.*" Believe in yourself.

An Older Person Has Several Advantages Starting a New Company

The startup environment is always very challenging. However, a person with significant business or professional experience can leverage their experience in several key areas. You can apply that professional experience to serve you well in the startup environment. By the time you reach the fifty-plus demographic, you've been around the block a few times, learned some hard lessons, and understand the importance of delivering value to your customers. People who join you in a startup will support the direction you take if you're appropriately transparent about the issues and involve the team in analyzing the pros and cons of major decisions.

The maturity and integrity you demonstrate will help you and your team execute the plan or revise the plan if it's not working. A key one includes the maturity to face setbacks and adversity calmly. And not panic. Your personnel recruiting, financial controls, and cash management experience can save you from the typical stress and mistakes encountered by young entrepreneurs. You have a sense of how your industry has grown over the years and you probably have a good perspective on where the industry will develop in the next five to ten years.

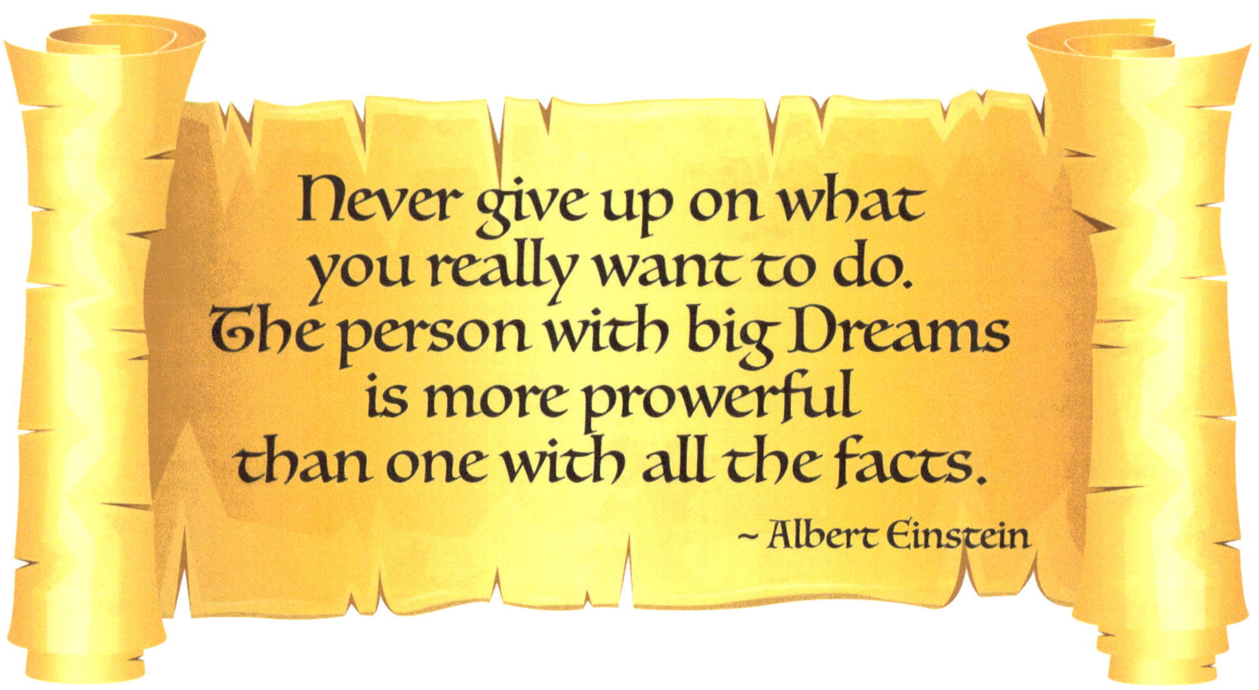

Nancy McKarney

Have you ever started out on a trek toward a dream, feeling hugely inspired and excited, only to lose momentum and throw in the towel? It could be because you have forgotten about your big picture reason for taking action—the vision that you are working toward and the sweet feelings of joy, fulfillment, or accomplishment you will experience in abundance once you have crossed the goal line. Keep reminders of your dream close by. When you lose focus, pause to reflect on what it would feel like to have already achieved your goal or dream in the here and now. Try to personify this feeling for a few minutes, and let it inspire a new wave of motivation inside you.

Dreams can take time to grow. Know exactly what you want. A dream starts with a to-the-point objective or intention. Dream with your heart and love with your soul. Once you have committed yourself to your dream, there is no telling what you will be able to achieve. No matter what stage of life you are in, the sky is the limit.

When you embrace your identity, you will discover a productive power you never imagined having that says *no* big picture is too big. It will take *patience*, long-term planning, and resilience. You must be willing to speak the languages of others, and you must walk in their shoes. Business is a tool to support what you believe in. Read books to widen your horizons. Know yourself better.

Don't pretend what you do doesn't shape your life. Your dream come true runs your entire life. Even if you work only eight hours a day, it still controls your life. What you wear and when you wake up and when you eat and when you come home and when you go to sleep are all scheduled around your work.

Keep an eye on the big picture. It's okay if you don't have it figured out as long as you don't stop figuring. Take responsibility for your big picture, even though it might have come in and out of focus a few times. The bigger the picture, the longer it takes. If you don't know where you're headed when you begin, it can take a couple of years.

"When you give up your dreams, it's a short walk to disappointment" (Touched By An Angel). Look around. The world is full of things that, according to naysayers, should never have happened. Isn't it high time someone got negative about negativity?

YES, IT IS!

Say *No* to *No*. Just say *No* to *No*, impossible, impractical, or no.
"Where there is no vision, the people perish" Proverbs 29:18 KJV.

- Vision Defined: A dream is a burning passion, a conviction at the conscience level. A dream desires to see things change.

FOUR THINGS THAT DESTROY DREAMS

- Insecurities swirl inside you.

- Doubt shouts at you.

- Bad decisions undermine you.

- Fear swallows you.

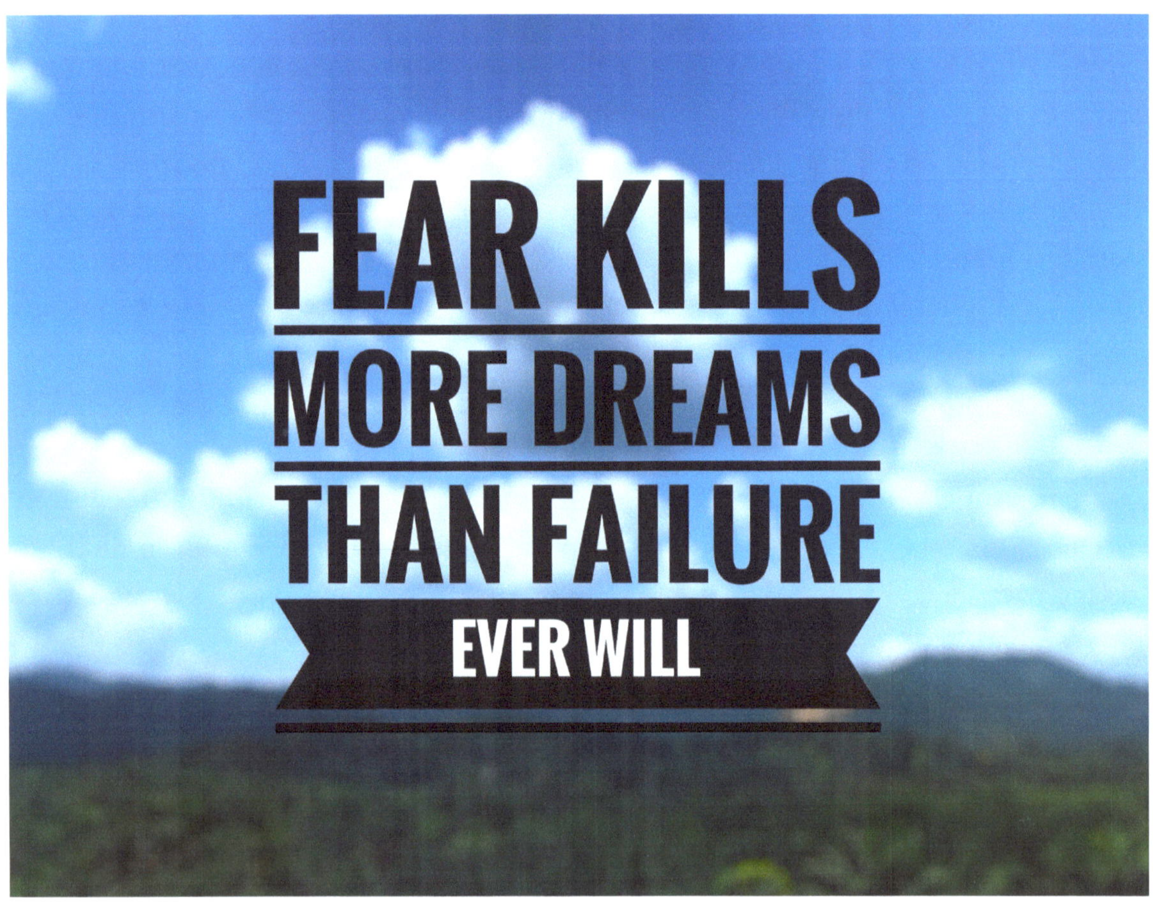

Shutterstock

To live a creative life, you must lose your fear of being wrong. Your dream is your road trip into the future. Let your *dream life* be bigger than your *fears*, your actions louder than your words, and your faith stronger than your feelings.

Three simple rules in life

1. If you do not go after what you want, you will never have it.
2. If you don't ask, the answer will always be no.
3. If you do not step forward, you'll always be in the same place.

PESSIMISTS WILL STALK YOU

*   The Alarmist says, "It's not safe!"
*   The Traditionalist says, "It's not the way we do it!"
*   The Defeatist says, "It's not possible!"
*   The Antagonist says, "I won't let you!"

AND YET *YES*

*   Yes, continents have been discovered.
*   Yes, men have played golf on the moon.
*   Yes, electricity is being turned into fuel to power cars.

YES, YES, YES

Just say *no* to *no* when the problem seems most unsolvable, when the challenge is hardest, and when everyone else is shaking their head, simply say, "*Let's go!*"

Walt Disney was an American entrepreneur, animator, writer, voice actor, and film producer. A pioneer of the American animation industry, he introduced several developments in the production of cartoons. As a film producer, Disney holds the record of most Academy Awards earned by an individual, having won twenty-two Oscars from fifty-nine nominations. He was presented with two Golden Globe Special Achievement Awards and an Emmy Award, among other honors. Several of his films are included in the National Film Registry by the Library of Congress.

Born in Chicago in 1901, Disney developed an early interest in drawing. He took art classes as a boy and got a job as a commercial illustrator at the age of eighteen. With animator Ub Iwerks, Walt developed the character Mickey Mouse in 1928, his first highly popular success; he also provided the voice for his creation in the early years. Disney became more adventurous, introducing synchronized sound, full-color three-strip Technicolor, feature-length cartoons, and technical developments in cameras. The results, seen in features, such as Snow White and the Seven Dwarfs (1937), Pinocchio, Fantasia (both 1940), Dumbo (1941), and Bambi (1942), furthered the development of animated film.

Disney was a shy, self-deprecating, and insecure man in private but adopted a warm and outgoing public persona. He had high standards and high expectations of those with whom he worked. He remains an important figure in the history of animation and in the cultural history of the United States, where he is considered a national cultural icon. His film work continues to be shown and adapted; his namesake studio and company maintains high standards in its production of popular entertainment, and the Disney amusement parks have grown in size and number to attract visitors in several countries.

WALT DISNEY PROCLAIMED,

"All of your dreams can come true—if you have the courage to pursue them." You don't have to have it all figured out to move forward. Just take the next step.

> A dream is not part of human nature that looks back and thinks about what might have been but looks forward to what might be. May you look forward to following your heart and build your *dream* into *reality.*

STEP BY STEP

DREAM BIG
BE AWESOME
CHEER UP
LOOSEN UP
GET REAL
BE STRONG
AIM HIGHER
LOVE MORE
LAUGH HARDER

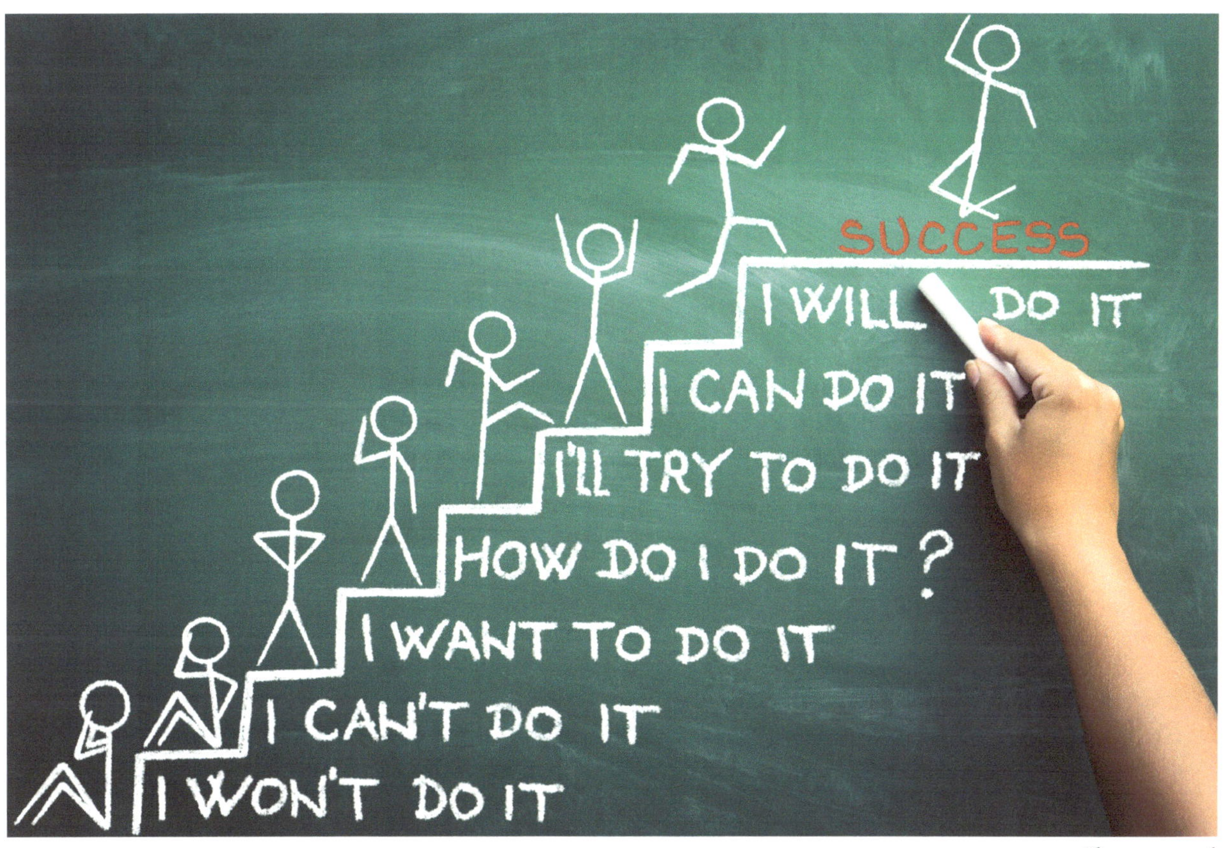

Shutterstock

Take responsibility for your life. This is the first and most important step toward making your dream life come true. Write it down so you capture it.

Chapter 7

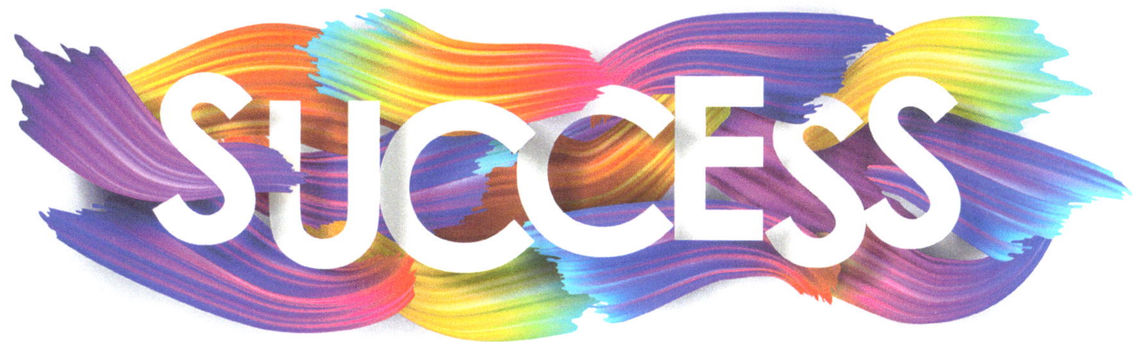

Shutterstock

Success is a journey, not a destination. Success doesn't happen on its own. Success at anything takes work, work, and then more work. Being a success means you have to get out there and hustle every day. Every day, you have to make the connections, do the tasks, deal with your to-do list, stay focused, and follow through, just to wake up and do it all over again the next day. But hard work pays off in the end. Some people succeed because they are destined to, but most people succeed because they are determined to. Desiring your dream life is valuable as you move forward on your journey to make it a dream come true. Desiring is valuable but work and desire are supreme.

Success is for anyone who will do what it takes to make it happen. The truth is that you can be successful if you set your mind to it and believe that you can. And by all means, stop comparing yourself to other people! Sometimes it's easy to get caught up in the success of others. When this happens, you usually start comparing your current situation to their high level of success. Often, you only see their success and don't see their early days of struggle.

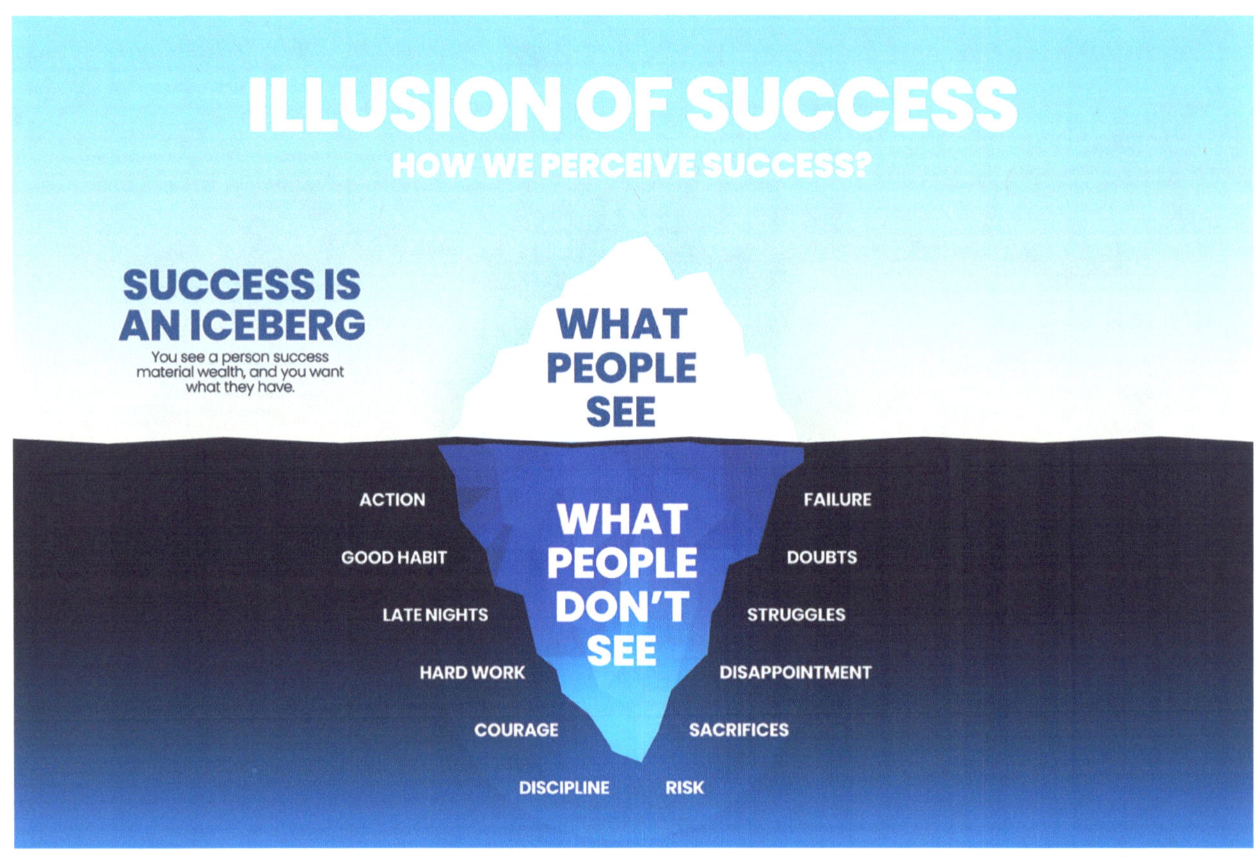

Shutterstock

If your life is like most folks', then there are probably some things in your past career that you're not too proud of. Regardless, your past is your past, and you must stop believing that your past can stop your success. Your past is behind you; that's why it's called your past. Quit looking back and start looking forward. Instead of being menaced by your past, decide to let your past be your present educator. Learn from it and become wiser in your venture to reach your dream life. Whatever you do, keep looking forward. Your determination will be the driving force that will get you through the hardships, setbacks, and difficult times that you will no doubt do battle with on your journey toward your dream life of success.

THE VALUE OF FAILURE

There will be moments when plans don't work out. Failure is an amazing trainer. There is a growing body of research that suggests that coming to grips with failure is essential for success. Of course, without the existence of failure, success would have no meaning. But the two terms aren't merely opposites. The more we learn about human striving, the more we see that success and failure are inextricably bound together. One study found that when people embraced and acknowledged their emotional response to failure, they tried harder next time. Failure is painful, and it doesn't make success inevitable. It is impossible to live without failing at something.

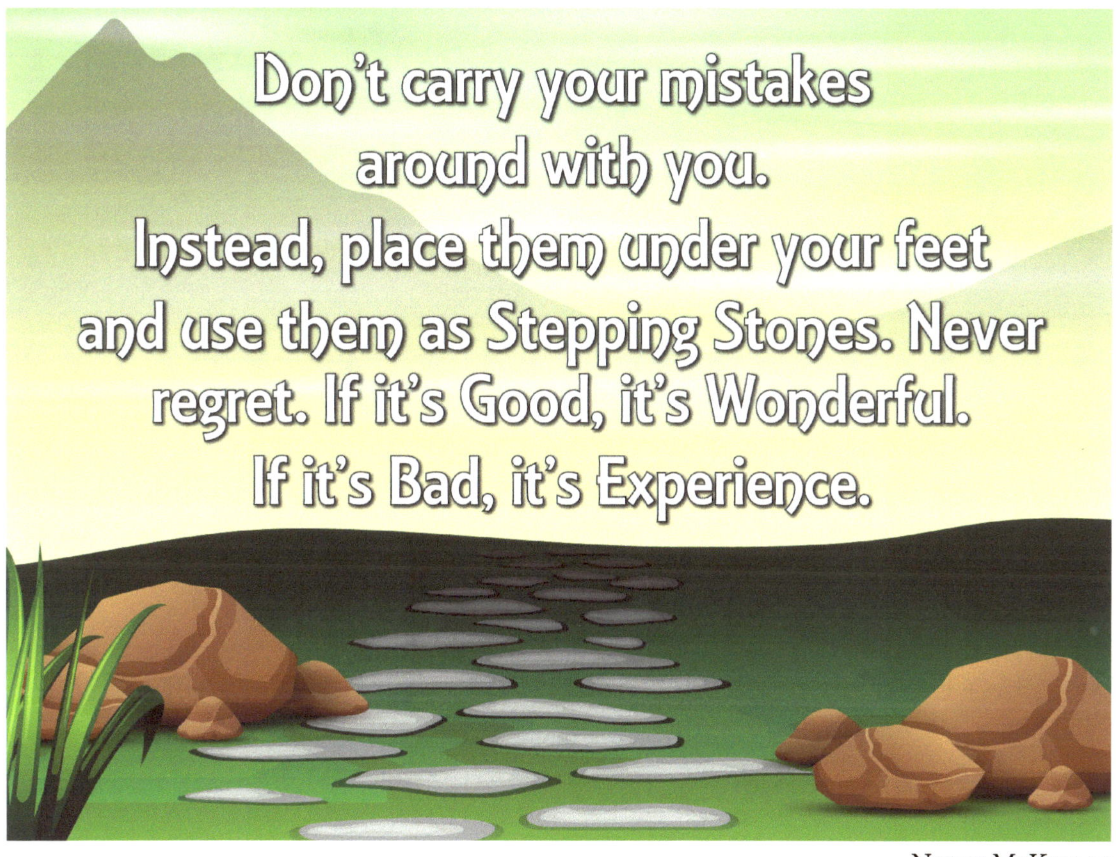

Nancy McKarney

Press On
Nothing in the world can take the place of persistence.

Talent Will Not-
Nothing is more common than unsuccessful people with talent

Genius Will Not-
Unrewarded genius is legendary.

Education Will Not-
The world is full of educated derelicts.

**Persistence & Determination Alone
Are Omnipotent**
-President Calvin Coolidge

Nancy McKarney

Some of history's most successful people were once duds who conquered failure with unyielding determination:

Fred Astaire (1899–1987) The dance legend received one of the most infamous screen-test rejections in Hollywood history. Wrote the studio executive: "Can't act. Slightly bald. Can dance a little."

Dr. Seuss (1904–1991) Born Theodor Geisel, the author of *The Cat in the Hat, How the Grinch Stole Christmas.* and other children's classics went for his Ph.D. in literature at Lincoln College, Oxford, but dropped out. His first book, *And to Think I Saw it on Mulberry Street,* was rejected twenty-seven times.

Sylvester Stallone (1946–present) At one point, Stallone was homeless, living for three weeks in the Port Authority Bus Terminal in New York. While writing *Rocky,* he sold his dog for $50 just to pay the rent.

Robert T. Kiyosaki (1947–present) He found monster success at fifty with his self-help best seller *Rich Dad, Poor Dad.* But Kiyosaki overcame plenty of setbacks—his company, which marketed the first nylon and Velcro surfer wallets, went bankrupt. So did his second, which made T-shirts, hats, wallets, and bags for heavy-metal bands.

Oprah Winfrey (1954–present) Born to a single teenage mother, she overcame soul-crushing challenges including childhood abuse. Winfrey ran away at thirteen, got pregnant at fourteen, and lost the baby shortly after birth. Yet she rose to become a TV anchor–only to be fired from her first job in Baltimore for being unfit for television news. Said Oprah, "It shook me to my very core."

Bill Gates (1955–present) Today the Microsoft mogul and tech pioneer is worth over $100 billion, but he easily might have become discouraged from the get-go; at seventeen, Gates and friends started a company called Traf-O-Data, which analyzed traffic logs—and it tanked.

> "When you were born you were given many tools. Throughout your life you learn how to use these tools. Some come naturally, some not. Some of these tools you use to build other tools. But this is for sure; Your life is a learning process to master all the tools in your toolbox. Do not give up on building your dream life! It's a matter of finding and mastering the right tools and learning as you go." —**Anna Pereira**

Sometimes the strength within you is not a big fiery flame for everyone to see; it's just a tiny spark that whispers ever so softly, "Keep going. You've got this!"

Your success can only be defined by you. But in order for me to help you think about it, we need a working definition that you can apply to your own situation.

Believe in yourself.
Believe in your dream.
Believe you have what it takes to be successful.
Believe that it's not too late.
Believe that your past is behind you, and your future is ahead of you.

You have the power and the ability to decide today and start the amazing journey of going from where you are to where you want to be. All you have to do is start.

TEN RULES FOR DEFINING SUCCESS

Rule 1: Your success is defined only by you
For that, we need to define ourselves. This involves knowing ourselves and what we want out of life.

Rule 2: Success is a feeling
How we feel about where we have been and where we are going is the ultimate test of our success in life, not the symbols of success.

Rule 3: Success at any price may not be success
The way in which you reach your goals has an impact on how you feel.

Rule 4: Success is a process
It is not the end point but the process of defining, redefining, struggling toward, and reaching the goals you set for your life.

Rule 5: Success occurs in steps
Expecting to find success in instant solutions invites lifelong disappointments. Success, like learning to walk, is a process that occurs in tiny steps.

Rule 6: Success is a balancing act
We all have a personal life, a relational life, and a work life. Balance, perspective, and trade-offs in these three areas are necessary for success and to prevent burnout.

Rule 7: Success can be learned

The ingredients of success are not inherited. Rather, they are learned traits that can be studied and changed.

Rule 8: Defining success too high or too low is a no-go

The best way to start defining and experiencing success is by setting up realistic goals that can be obtained in a reasonable amount of time. This also leads to greater goals.

Rule 9: Success is being able to be honest with yourself

Success requires honesty; otherwise, you will feel like an imposter.

Rule 10: Treat Others Well

Your smile is your logo; your personality is your business card. How you leave others feeling after having an experience with you becomes your trademark.

Love the life you live;
live the life you love.

You have a CHOICE
Each and Every Single Day.
I Choose to feel BLESSED.
I CHOOSE to feel GRATEFUL.
I CHOOSE to be EXCITED.
I CHOOSE to be THANKFUL.
I CHOOSE to be HAPPY.

Nancy McKarney

DESIGN YOUR LIFE

You do not get what you want until you know what you want. What do you want in your life? Well, start looking by visualizing the completed goal. Following is a questionnaire that will help you determine exactly what you want out of your life.

- What would I like to accomplish before I die?

- What do I want to own that I do not currently own?

- What kind of car do I really want to drive?

- What kind of house do I want to live in?

- At which stores do I really want to shop?

- What kind of clothes would I like to wear?

- Which restaurants do I want to go to?

- Where would I like to travel?

- How would I like to spend my recreational time?

- Which people would I like to spend time with?

- What would I really like to do if time and money were not issues?

- How much money would I like to earn each year?

- How much money would I like to have saved/invested?

- How much money would I like to give away each year?

What kind of relationships do I WANT?

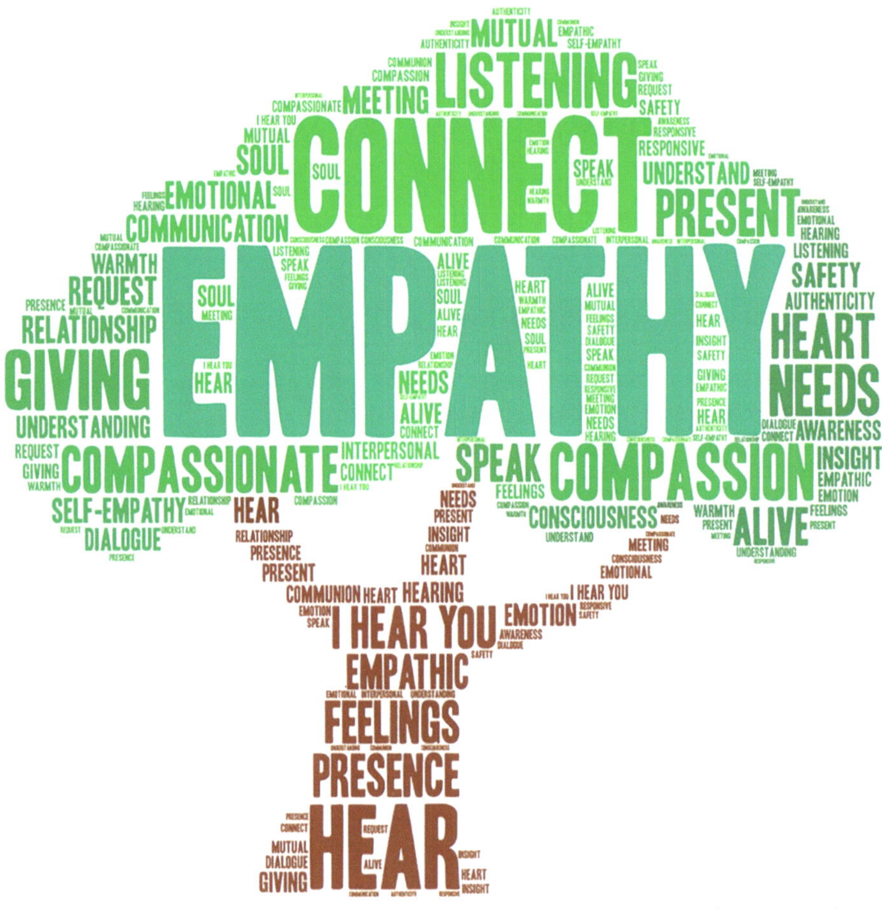

Shutterstock

- **With my spouse/significant other/partner/lover/special friend?**

  - **With my children?**

  - **With my family?**

  - **With my co-workers?**

  - **With my friends?**

  - **With God?**

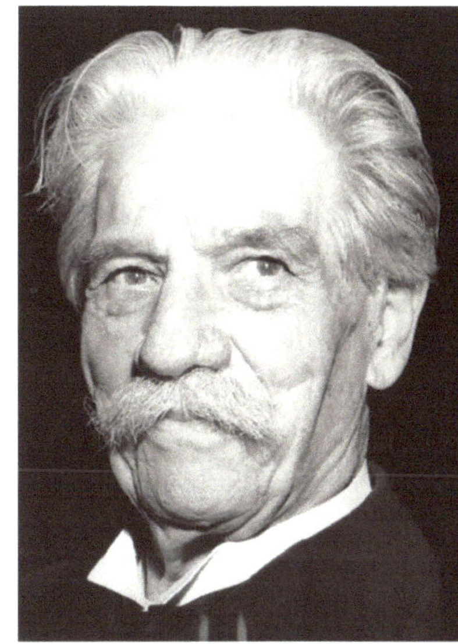

Shutterstock

VISUALIZE YOUR PERFECT LIFE

The Three C's of Life

Choices

Chances

Changes

You must make a choice to take a chance to change your life.

What am I doing to make this happen?

What am I *really* doing to create the life I want?

Chapter 8

Launch Your Dream

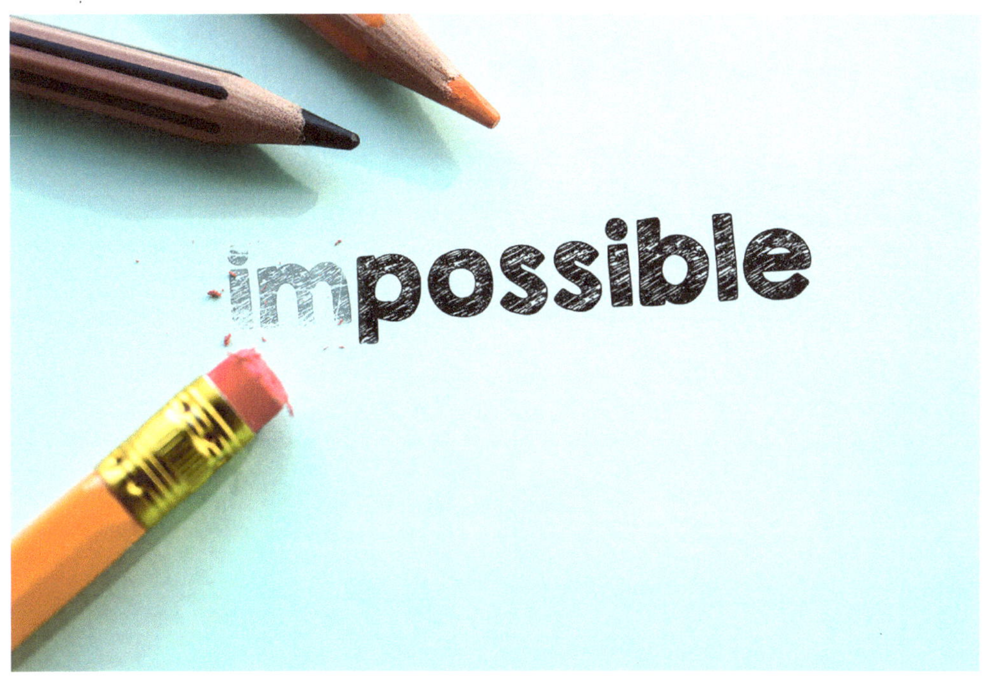

Shutterstock

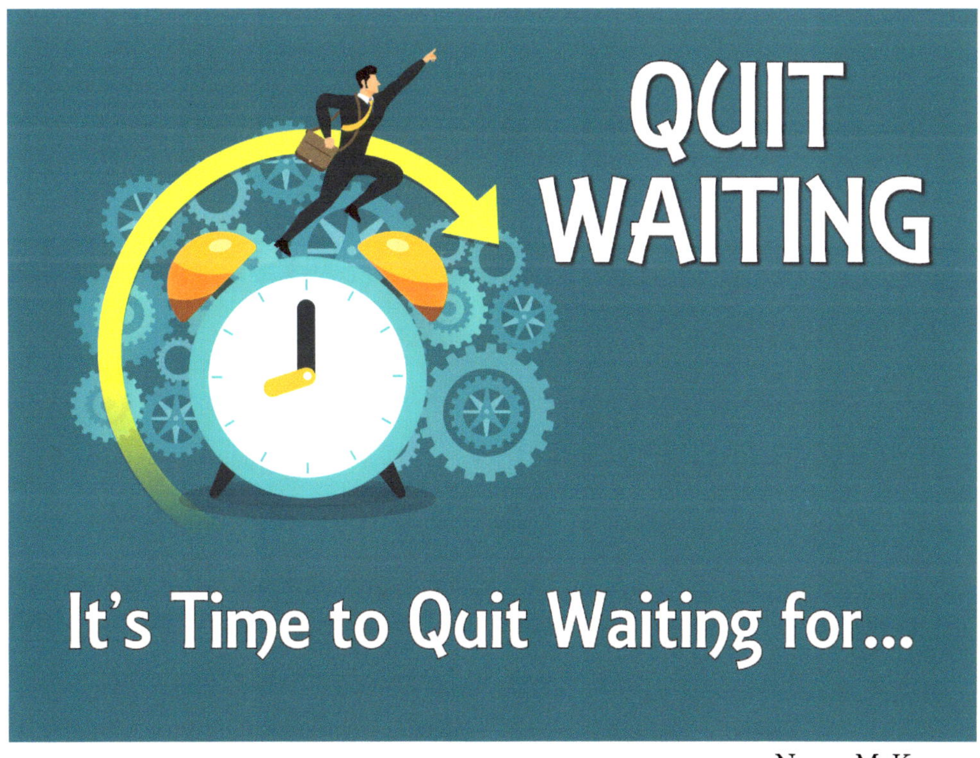

Nancy McKarney

- Perfection
- Inspiration
- Permission
- Reassurance
- Someone to change
- The right person to come along
- The kids to leave home
- A more favorable horoscope
- The administration to take over
- An absence of risk
- Someone to discover you
- A clear set of instructions
- More Self-confidence
- The pain to go away

LAUNCH YOUR DREAM

Over time, as a result of my life and business experiences, I have learned the word *dream* is interchangeable with the word *goal*. When one chooses to act on a

dream, it transforms from a nursery rhyme like "Star Light, Star Bright" into a definitive goal with the possibility of becoming a reality. I repeat, the words dreams, and goals are interchangeable. Dreams become goals when acted upon, and goals realized are dreams come true. Without the *desire*, a call to action, the dream is no more than wishful thinking. The moment a person desires a dream to come true, the dream begins the process of metamorphosis. By acting on the desire, the dream becomes a goal.

But that is not enough to manifest the dream into reality. *Determination,* blood, sweat, and tears are the nutrients that make the dream grow. Doing the pick-and-shovel work and heavy lifting is still not enough to make a dream a reality. It also requires *discipline* to see it through. When you have a setback, fall down, are overcome by circumstances beyond your control, or get rejected, you must have the resiliency to bounce back, ever moving forward, to break through the wall to the other side to become a *dream achiever*.

REALITY CHECK. For unknown reasons not all dreams come true, as we imagine. The good news is found in the words of **Friedrich Nietzsche "What does not kill me only makes me stronger."**

THE FOUR D'S not only work in a person's life to realize wishes and hope of professional success and life prosperity, but they also work to overcome personal obstacles and hardships:

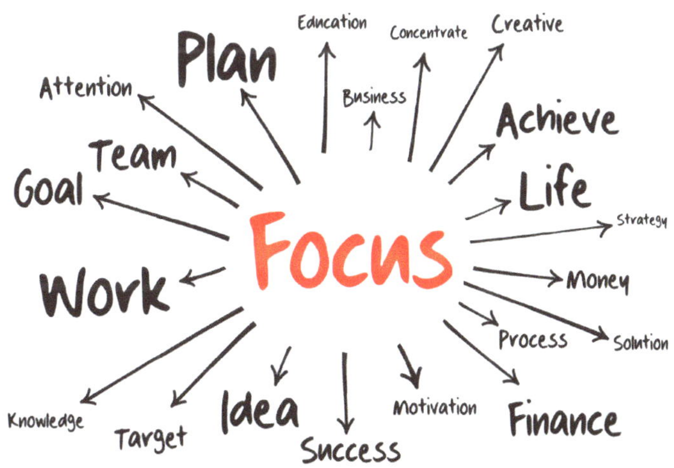

Shutterstock

❖ **DREAMS**—We all have them.

❖ **DESIRE**—Is the incubator starting the process to make a dream come true.

❖ **DECISION**—Sprouts the seed.

❖ **DISCIPLINE**—Brings readiness to become a dream achiever.

Having a life dream, professional or personal, can be daunting. Dreams never sleep. Hope and aspirations don't go away unless they are discarded and/or killed. Being a dreamer is not hard when you have witnessed up close and personal one of America's utmost dreamers realize his *big dream*. My childhood home was in Anaheim, California, two city blocks from Disneyland, The Magic Kingdom. My father was chief of Park Security and Communications at Disneyland.

A forty-acre orange grove separated my childhood home from "The Happiest Place on Earth," opened in 1955, when Walt Disney was fifty-four years of age. Employees called Disneyland "the park." For me, it was much more. It was, as Sam Spade said, *"the stuff that dreams are made of."* My father's position allowed me to go to Disneyland any time I wished. I had a book of "E-Tickets" and a child's delight in the park. I knew absolutely every inch of the amusement park. My first jobs—selling ice cream on Main Street and working in the malt shop in Frontierland—were at Disneyland.

As a teenager in the early 1960s, I went to weekly Saturday night dances at the park during the summers. I enjoyed the beautiful Christmas season at Disneyland, where Walt Disney turned the whole park into an illuminated, sparkling, magical winter wonderland. And every night in the summer months, we watched from our front porch as the nightly Disneyland fireworks magnificently ended another day at the park. My life—my world—was the Wonderful World of Disney. I met Walt Disney three times during my frequent escapades to the park. Once was when I was with my father as Walt strolled along Main Street, something he often did. The other two times were at employee events, like the Christmas party. I remember him being very nice to me, with a warm smile and a distinct twinkle in his eye. Because of my childhood experience, I have been a dreamer throughout my youth and adult life. I assume you're a dreamer too, or you wouldn't be reading this Workbook.

Chapter 9

Career and Business Planning

USPS POSTAGE STAMP

"The way to get started is to quit talking and begin doing." —Walt Disney

The expert in anything
was once a beginner.

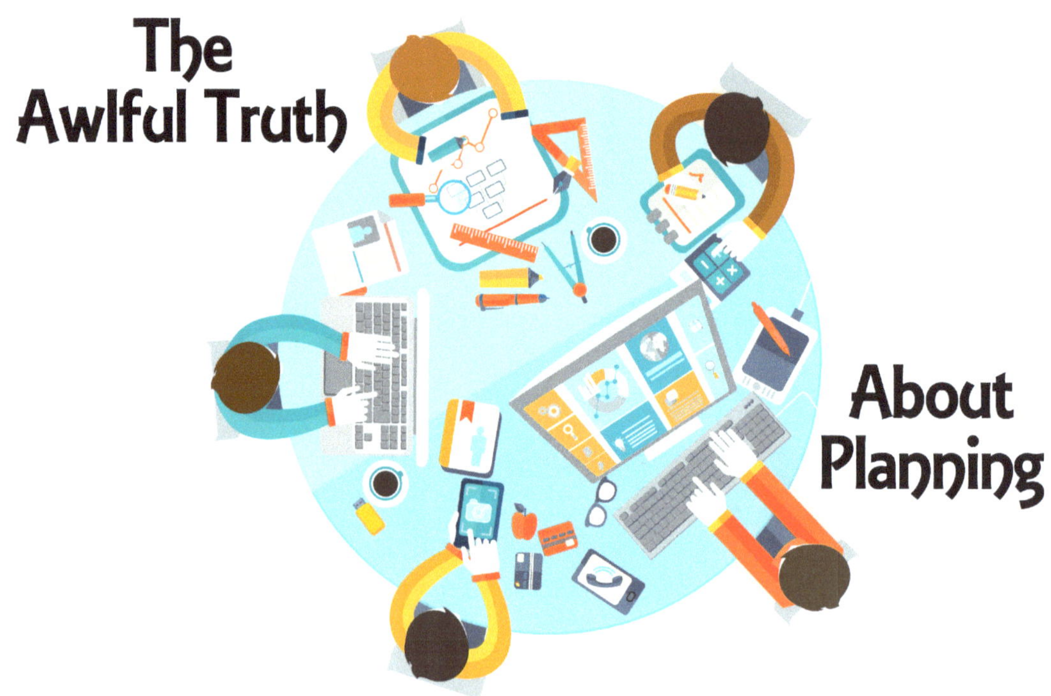

Nancy McKarney

The Awful Truth About Planning

- **Plans are pure fiction.**
- **There never was one that happened the way it was written.**
- **At the same time, planning is a smart thing to do because it gets you into action.**
- **Action provides you with many happy accidents.**
- **While you're calling people, looking things up in the Yellow pages, even if you find yourself in one blind alley after another, you're sure to stumble on unexpected opportunity.**

The Awful Truth About Planning

- **The very unpredictability of life turns into an asset because you don't have to have all the answers, just the general direction and a willingness to show up. Woody Allen said, "80% of success is showing up."**
- **When you start planning steps on paper, wishful thinking does an about face and becomes a to-do list, just as real as a grocery shopping.**
- **A plan gets you out of your head and into the world, where reality will provide the pieces to your puzzle.**

The Awful Truth About Planning

- **This is the pivotal point or a real transformation.**
- **When dreams don't make it to the planning stage, they stay in the clouds, never to become reality.**
- **When plans push you into action, however, all kinds of benefits flood into your life.**
- **Alone with your dreams you think you have to create everything on your own: out in the world you find much will come to meet you.**

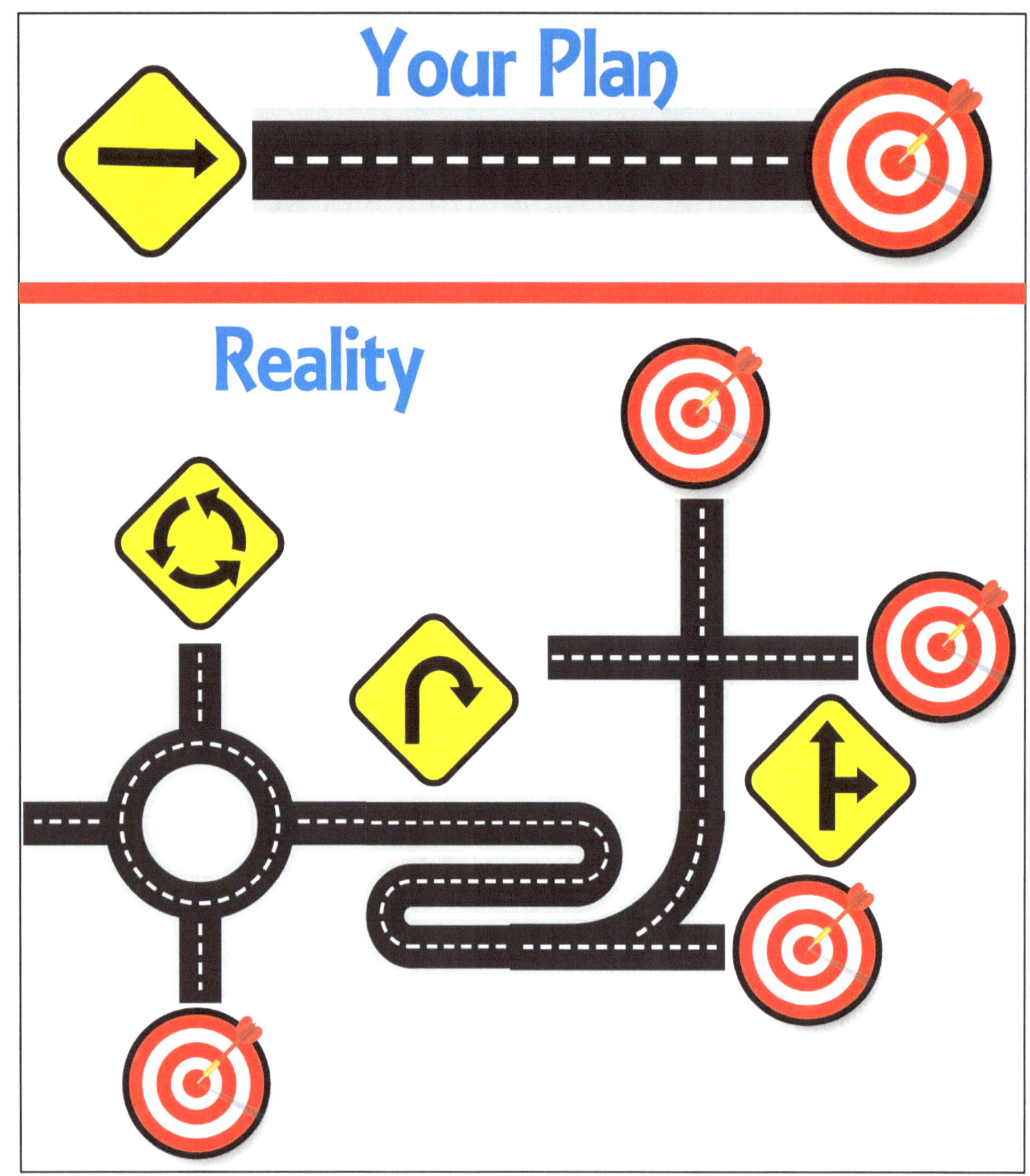

Nancy McKarney

Twists & turns only mean that the way is difficult, not that the destination is unreachable. YOUR POSITION IS ALL

IN PEOPLE'S MINDS.

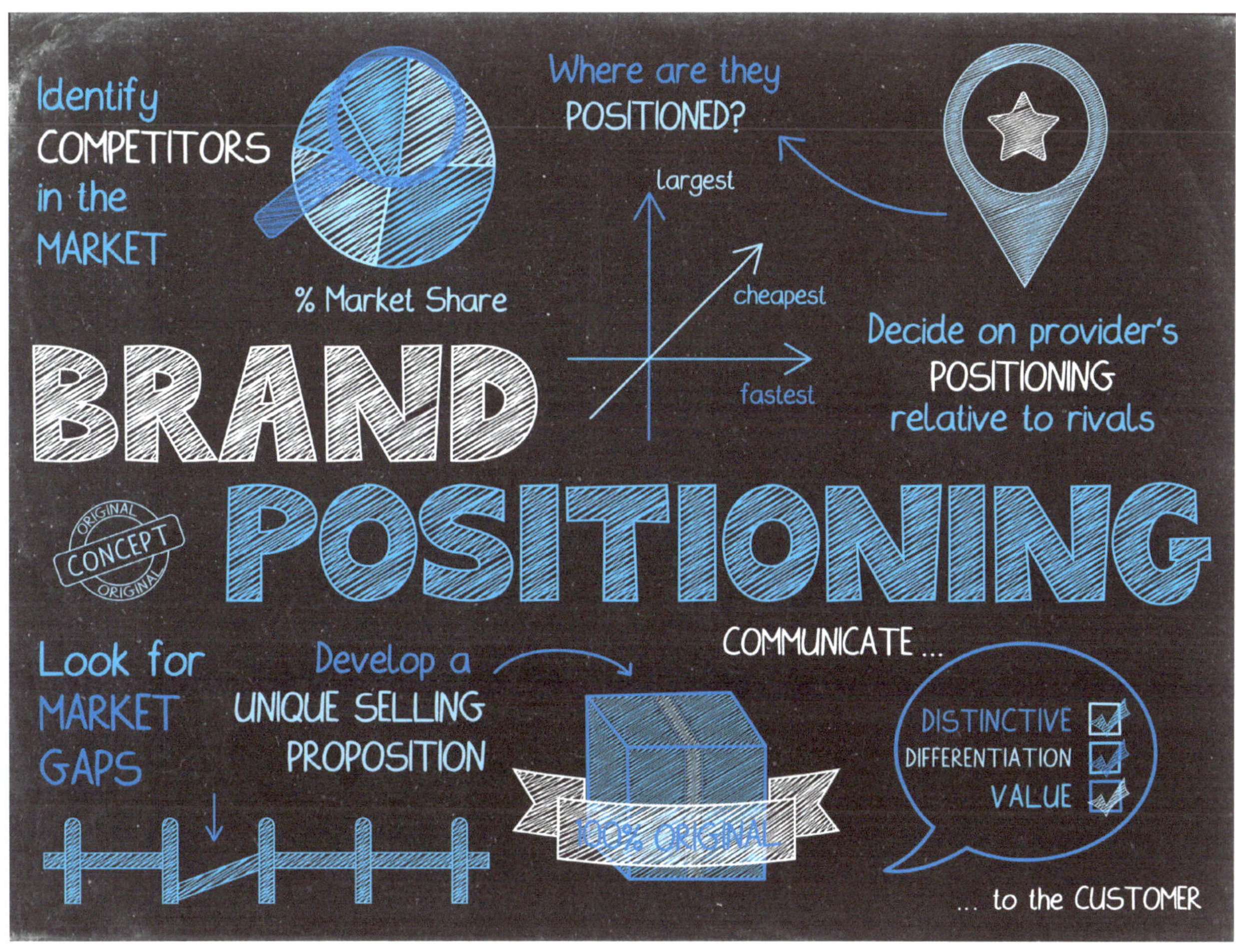

Shutterstock

FIND OUT WHAT THAT POSITION IS.

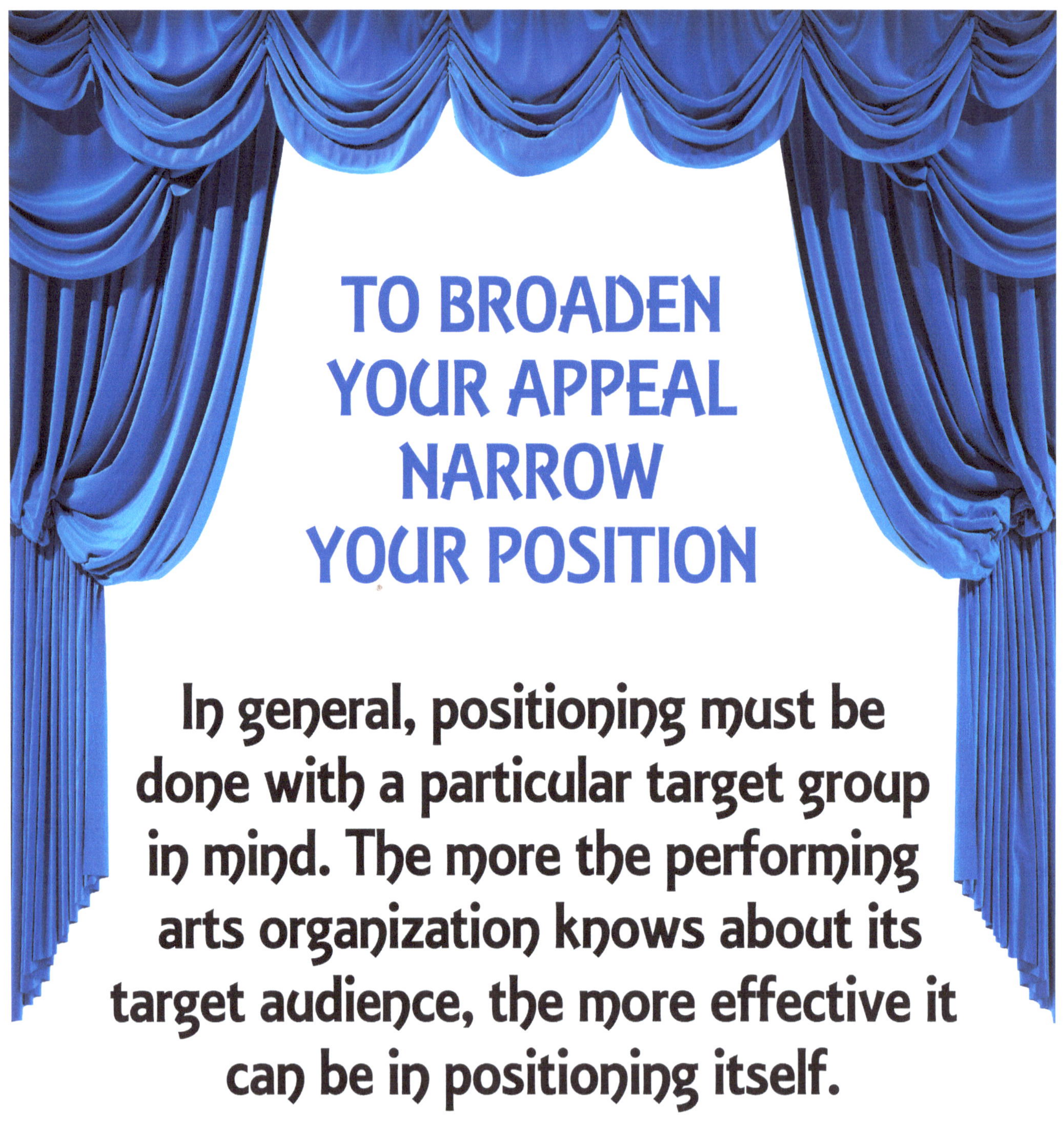

TO BROADEN
YOUR APPEAL
NARROW
YOUR POSITION

In general, positioning must be done with a particular target group in mind. The more the performing arts organization knows about its target audience, the more effective it can be in positioning itself.

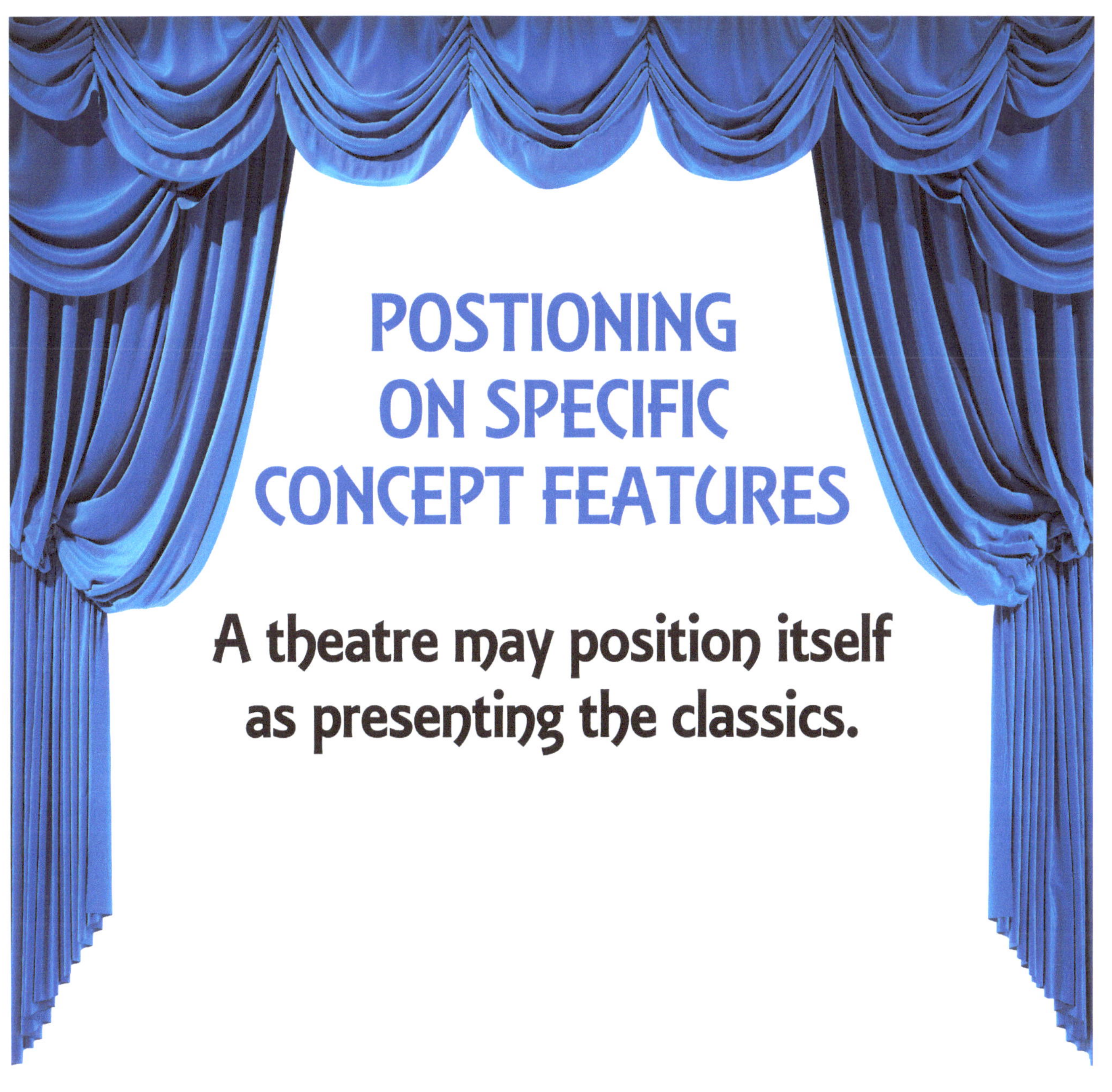
POSTIONING
ON SPECIFIC
CONCEPT FEATURES

A theatre may position itself
as presenting the classics.

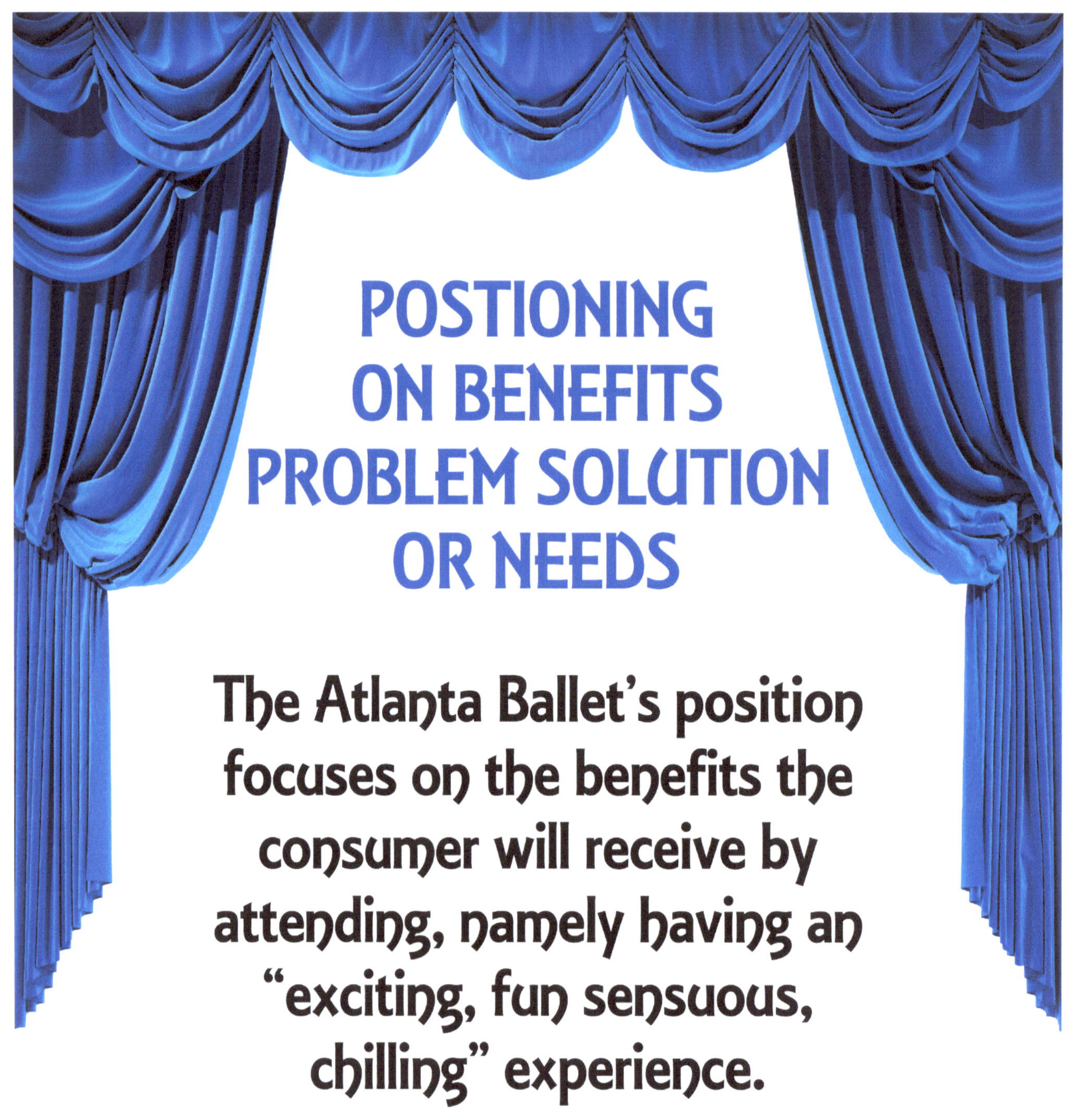

POSTIONING
ON BENEFITS
PROBLEM SOLUTION
OR NEEDS

The Atlanta Ballet's position focuses on the benefits the consumer will receive by attending, namely having an "exciting, fun sensuous, chilling" experience.

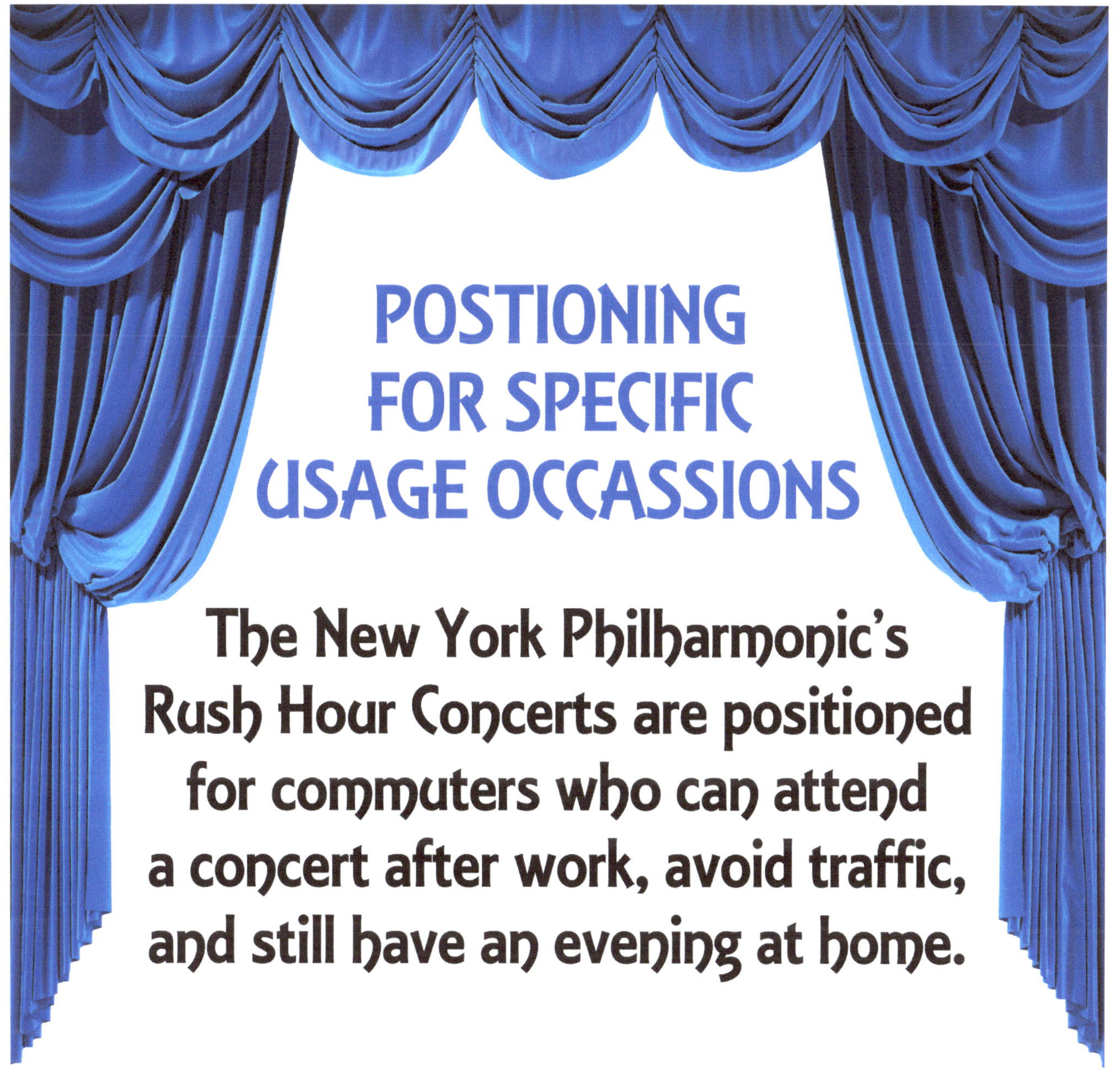
POSTIONING
FOR SPECIFIC
USAGE OCCASSIONS

The New York Philharmonic's
Rush Hour Concerts are positioned
for commuters who can attend
a concert after work, avoid traffic,
and still have an evening at home.

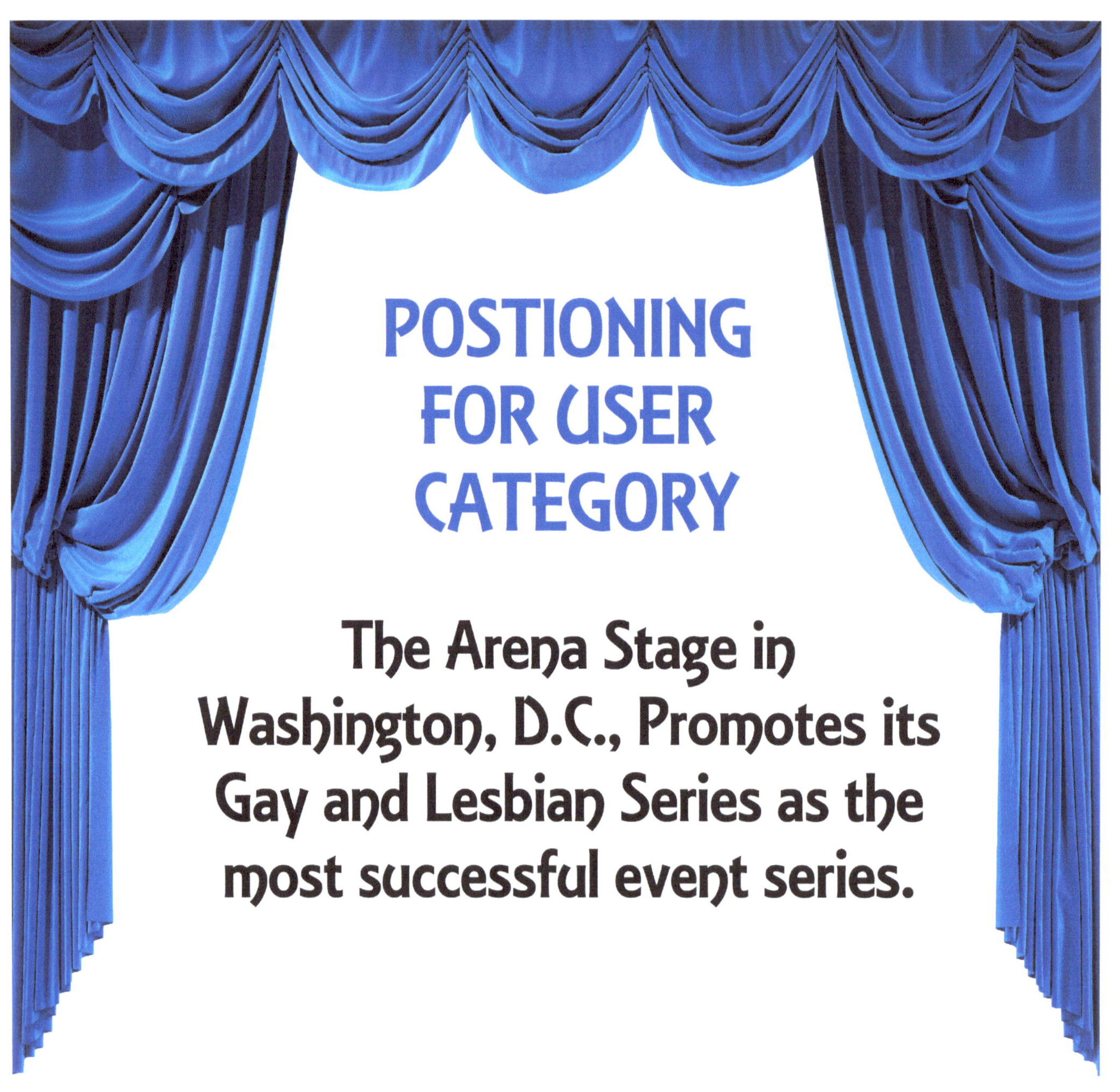

POSTIONING
FOR USER
CATEGORY

The Arena Stage in
Washington, D.C., Promotes its
Gay and Lesbian Series as the
most successful event series.

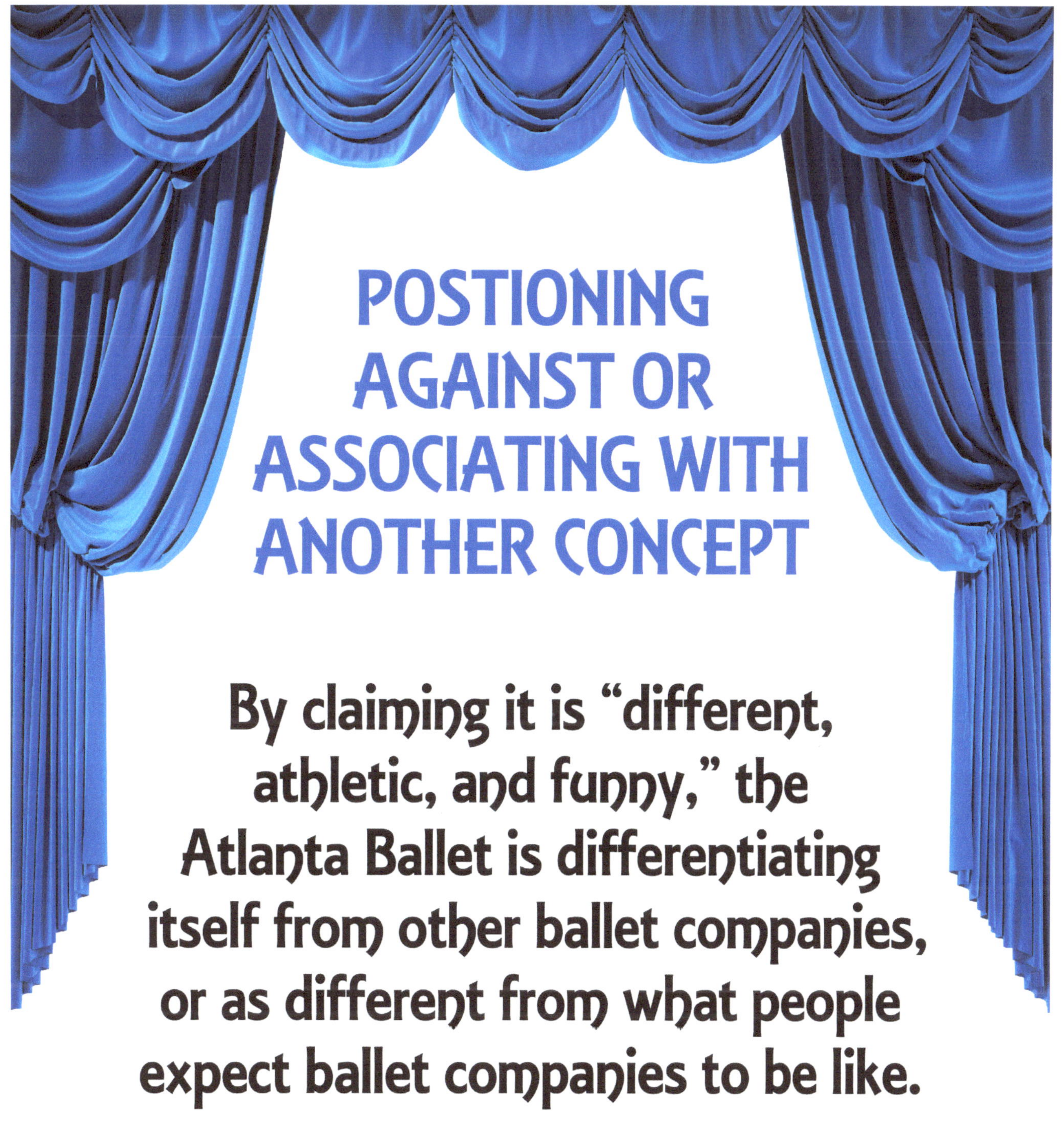
POSTIONING
AGAINST OR
ASSOCIATING WITH
ANOTHER CONCEPT

By claiming it is "different,
athletic, and funny," the
Atlanta Ballet is differentiating
itself from other ballet companies,
or as different from what people
expect ballet companies to be like.

POSTIONING AS NUMBER ONE

People tend to remember number one and to value it much more highly than any other offering or person that may be a close runner-up. For example, when asked, "who was the first person to successfully fly across the Atlantic Ocean?" we will answer "Charles Lindberg. When asked, "Who was the second person to do it?" We draw a blank.

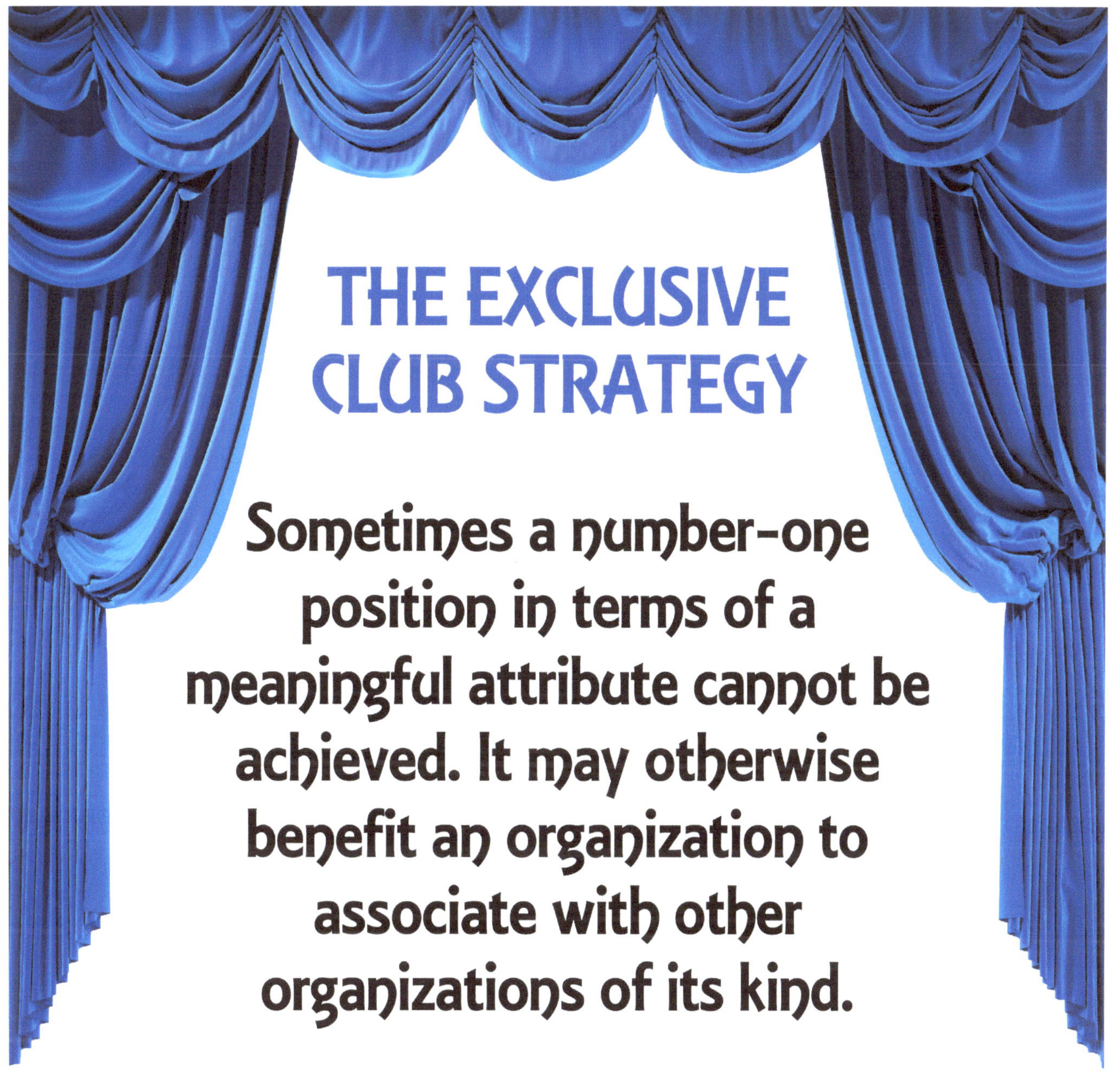

THE EXCLUSIVE
CLUB STRATEGY

Sometimes a number-one
position in terms of a
meaningful attribute cannot be
achieved. It may otherwise
benefit an organization to
associate with other
organizations of its kind.

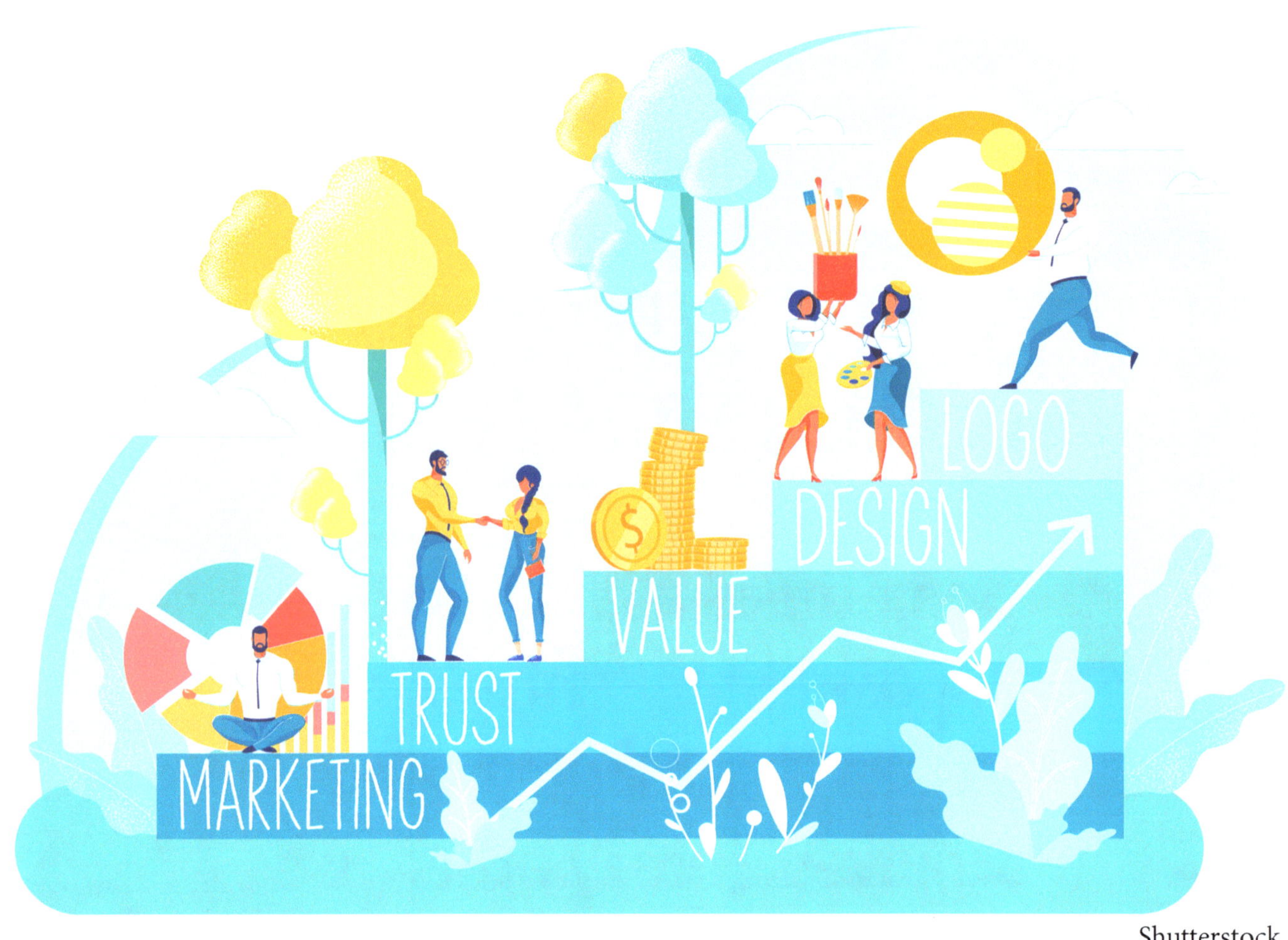

Shutterstock

MARKET SEGMENTATION

Market segments are groups of customers that have similar buying characteristics. Identify your target market(s).

- ✓ Teenagers
- ✓ Senior citizens
- ✓ Women 18–45

DEMOGRAPHIC

- ✓ Age
- ✓ Income
- ✓ Race
- ✓ Sex
- ✓ Marital status

GEOGRAPHICAL

- ✓ Climate
- ✓ Regions
- ✓ Counties
- ✓ Cities
- ✓ Neighborhoods

PSYCHOGRAPHIC

- ✓ Personality characteristics
- ✓ Attitudes
- ✓ Beliefs
- ✓ Opinions
- ✓ Lifestyle

SPIROGRAPHICS

- ❖ Simply defined, *spirographics* is the intricate web of religious, mystical, or spiritual insights, feelings, experiences, and preferences which serve as the foundation of an individual's or group's motivation.

- ❖ A spirographic profile can find people and communicate with them, based on their spiritual orientation.

- ❖ Like every group, believers and near-believers need their values to be reinforced.

- ❖ It is impossible to understand religious America's similarities and differences without understanding intimately and personally the life-changing message to which many of these people depend on.

Demographics define **who** a person is.

Psychographics describes **what** a person is like.

Spirographics explains the **why** a person does what they do.

POSITIONING

- ❖ You must position yourself in your prospect's mind.

- ❖ Your position should be singular: one simple message.

- ❖ Your position must set you apart from your competitors.

- ❖ You must sacrifice. You cannot be all things to all people; you must focus on one thing.

The Oversimplified Message

❖ In communication, as in architecture, less is more.

❖ You have to sharpen your message to cut into the mind.

❖ You have to jettison the ambiguities, simplify the message, and then simplify it some more if you want to make a long-lasting impression.

What Position Do You Own?

❖ Positioning is thinking in reverse. Instead of starting with yourself, you start with the mind of the prospect. Instead of asking what you are, you ask what position you already own or want to own in the mind of the prospect.

What Position Do You Want to Own?

❖ Here is where you bring out your crystal ball and try to figure out the best position to own from a long-term point of view. *Own* is the key word. Too many programs set out to communicate a position that is impossible to establish because someone else already owns it.

To Broaden Your Appeal, Narrow Your Position.

❖ Position is a passive noun, not an active verb.

❖ No company can position itself as anything. You can focus your efforts and your message, which sometimes can influence your position. But your position is a place, and your prospects put you there.

❖ Even services that do nothing to market their company have a position. A prospect simply takes what he knows about the company and positions the company accordingly.

Creating Your Positioning Statement

❖ Before you create a positioning statement, one warning: Don't confuse a position with a positioning statement.

❖ A position (or statement of position) is a cold-hearted, no-nonsense statement of how you are perceived in the minds of prospects. It is your position.

❖ A positioning statement, by contrast, states how you wish to be perceived. It is the core message you want to deliver in every medium to influence the perception of your product or service.

What Position Do You Own?

❖ Positioning is thinking in reverse. Instead of starting with yourself, you start with the mind of the prospect. Instead of asking what you are, you ask what position you already own or want to own in the mind of the prospect.

Who Must You Outgun?

❖ If your proposed position calls for a head-to-head approach against a marketing leader, forget it. It's better to go around an obstacle rather than face it head on. Try to select a position that no one else has firm grip on.

❖ Coming to grips with the competition is also the main problem in most marketing situations.

Do You Have Enough Money?

❖ A big obstacle to successful positioning is attempting to achieve the impossible. It takes money to build a share of mind. It takes money to establish a position. It takes money to hold a position once you've established it.

❖ With a given number of dollars, it's better to overspend in one city than to underspend in several cities. If you become successful in one location, you can always roll out the program to other places, provided the first location is appropriate.

❖ Example: If you become the No. 1 scotch in New York (the No.1 scotch-drinking area of the country), you can roll out the product to the rest of the USA.

Can You Stick It Out?

❖ You can think of our over-communicated society as a constant crucible of change, as one idea replaces another in bewildering succession.

❖ To cope with change, it's important to take a long-range point of view to determine your basic position and then stick to it.

❖ Positioning is a concept that is cumulative, something that takes advantage of advertising's long-range nature.

Do You Match Your Position?

❖ Creative people often resist positioning thinking because they believe it restricts their creativity. And you know what? It does. Positioning thinking does restrict creativity.

❖ One of the great communication tragedies is to watch an organization go through a careful planning exercise, step by step, complete with charts and graphs, and then turn the strategy over to the "creatives" for execution. They, in turn, apply their skills, and strategy disappears in a cloud of techniques, never to be recognized again.

- ❖ Do your advertisements for yourself match your position? Do your clothes, for example, tell the world that you're a banker, a lawyer, or an artist?

- ❖ Do you wear creative clothes that undermine your position?

- ❖ Creativity by itself is worthless. Only when it is subordinated to the positioning objectives can creativity contribute.

- ❖ With rare exceptions, a company should almost never change its basic positioning strategy, only its tactics, those short-term maneuvers that are intended to implement a long-term strategy.

- ❖ The trick is to take the basic strategy and improve it. Find new ways to dramatize it—new ways to avoid the boredom factor.

- ❖ Owning a position in the mind is like owning a valuable piece of real estate. Once you give it up, you might find it's impossible to get it back again.

The Power of the Name

- ❖ The name is the hook that hangs the brand on the product ladder in the prospect's mind. In the positioning era, the single most important marketing decision you can make is what to name the product or service.

- ❖ A strong, generic-like, descriptive name will block your me-too competitors from muscling their way into your territory. A good name is the best insurance for long-term success. *People* is a brilliant name for a gossip-column magazine. It's a runaway success. The me-too copy, *Us* magazine, is in trouble.

- ❖ Names also get out of date, opening up crevasses for alert competitors. With marginal differences in many product categories, a better name can mean millions of dollars of difference in sales.

Value Is Not a Position

❖ If your primary selling position is good value, you have no position.

❖ Value is not a competitive position. Value is what every service promises, implicitly or explicitly. It is fundamental to survival. A service's price must fairly reflect its value to the customer, or the service eventually will fail.

❖ Some legal services charge $50 for an uncontested divorce.

❖ Lawyer Lawrence Tribe charges $750 an hour.

❖ Acme's clients say they get good value.

However, most clients and experts point to Tribe's results—a 15–6 winning record before the US Supreme Court—and they say he gives very good value, too.

❖ In services, value is a given, and givens are not viable competitive positions.

❖ *If good value is the first thing you communicate, you won't be effective.*

Pricing: A Lesson from Picasso

❖ What is talent and thought worth—and why are they worth so much? What can you reasonably charge? Good questions. Before you answer them, consider this story about Pablo Picasso.

A woman was strolling along a street in Paris when she spotted Picasso sketching at a sidewalk café. So thrilled that she could not be slightly presumptuous, the woman asked Picasso if he might sketch her, and charge accordingly.

Picasso obliged. In just minutes, there she was: an original Picasso.

"And what do I owe you?" she asked.

"Five thousand francs," he answered.

"But it only took you three minutes," she politely reminded him.

"No," Picasso said. "It took me all my life."

❖ *Don't charge by the hour: Charge by the years.*

You can establish your position by answering the following questions:

❖ **Who:** Who are you?

❖ **What:** What business are you in?

❖ **For whom:** What people do you serve?

❖ **What need:** What are the special needs of the people you serve?

❖ **Against whom:** With whom are you competing?

❖ **What's different:** What makes you different from those competitors?

❖ **So:** What's the benefit? What unique benefit does a client derive from your service?

Ask yourself these seven questions—and have seven good, clear answers.

Creating Your Position Statement

A *positioning statement* describes what you want the world to think. A *statement of position*, by contrast, admits the truth. For most services, this statement of position basically reads:

Who	John Doe Inc.
What	is a small service company
For whom	that serves smaller clients who want pretty good quality but cannot pay, or do not want to pay, for the services of a larger company.
Against whom	Unlike it's bigger and better-known competitors,
What's different?	John Doe is smaller, less experienced, and not as outstanding. (Remember, this is the typical prospect's perception, and not necessarily reality.)
So,	but because of that, they charge less, so you can save some money.

❖ This is the position of 90 percent of all service companies because this is how they are perceived by potential customers.

❖ Chances are that this, or some slightly improved version, is your position statement. This is where you must start.

So, ask yourself, your clients, and your prospects,

"What is our position?"

Chapter 10

Goals Are Dreams with Deadlines

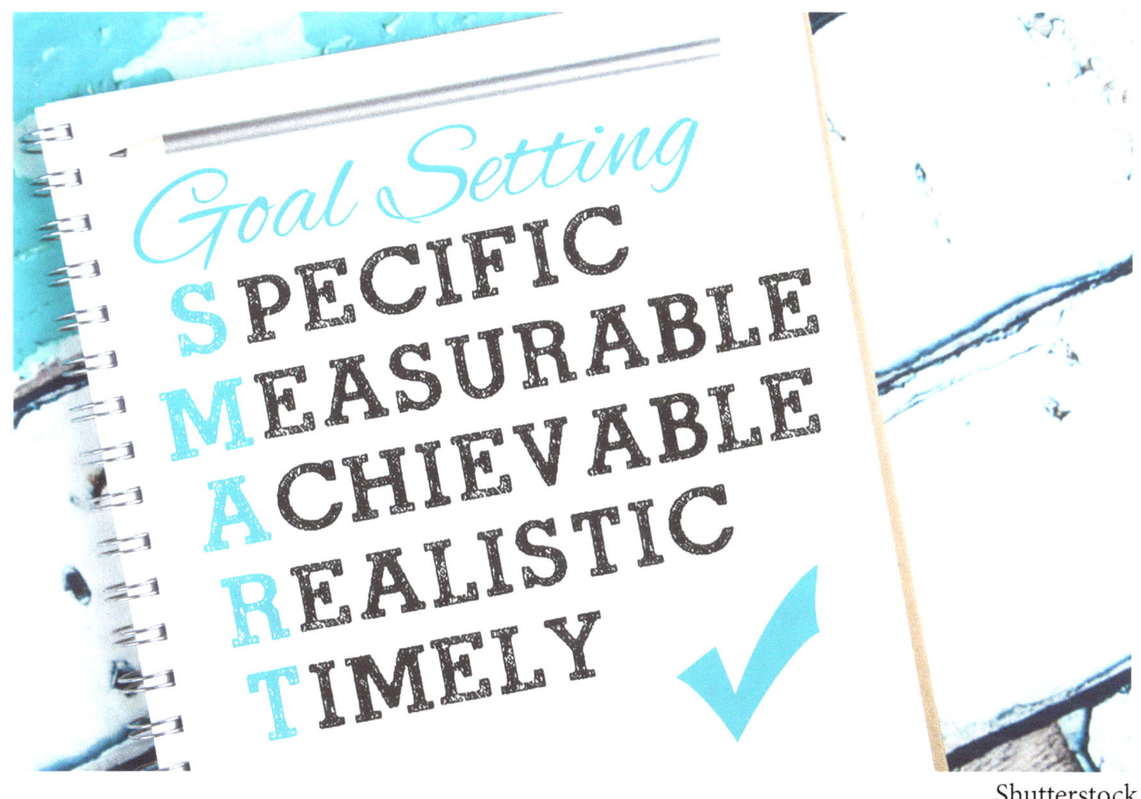

Shutterstock

Accomplishing goals with straightforwardness is an art that many people have yet to master. Goals should be *SMART*. This acronym, borrowed from the business world, stands for *"specific, measurable, achievable, realistic, and time-based."*

A key strategy for building SMART goals is to break a large goal into smaller pieces. By doing that and setting smaller targets, the goal is within reach, and yet it's still a challenge. Achieving smaller goals can help push you forward to the next step. If you can set a goal and achieve it, you get a boost in your motivation and a general good feeling about yourself and the world you are living in.

As you learned in Chapter 1, knowing your personal *values* is of the utmost importance in everyday living. *Align Your Goals with Your Values*. Know why a goal is meaningful to you.

It's important to ask yourself, "How does this fit into the bigger picture in my life, why am I doing this, is it really a goal that is based on a value I have, and is it something I feel I must do?

Ensuring that your goals are in line with who you are—and especially who you want to be—makes it much easier to stay committed to these goals and to ultimately achieve them.

Dreams and projects can take time to develop. If you're constantly and enthusiastically checking for evidence that your desires are on their way to maturing and everything is going precisely to plan, you may end up feeling anxious and discouraged. You may need to check in with your progress toward your goals and revise your plan every now and then but do it with determination at advantageous intervals.

There will almost certainly be slips or slip-ups on the path to achieving your goals, and the important thing is to not beat yourself up about them. We all have that inner voice that comments on what we're doing and how we're doing it. View any bumps along the way as chances to reassess and readjust your plans. Maybe you need to modify the goal a little bit, but you also need to look at the failure as a learning opportunity.

When you're working to realize your life dream goals, you are likely to encounter obstacles and face resistance. There are ways to face these challenges and make your life dream goals a reality. Anyone who wants to accomplish a *big goal* will encounter obstacles. That is natural. Anytime you try to do something outside the norm, you will face resistance. Not only will the world present challenges, but you can even experience resistance from your own mind. While talent and hard work are helpful on the road to success, the most important skill is the ability to overcome the obstacles that you will face along the way.

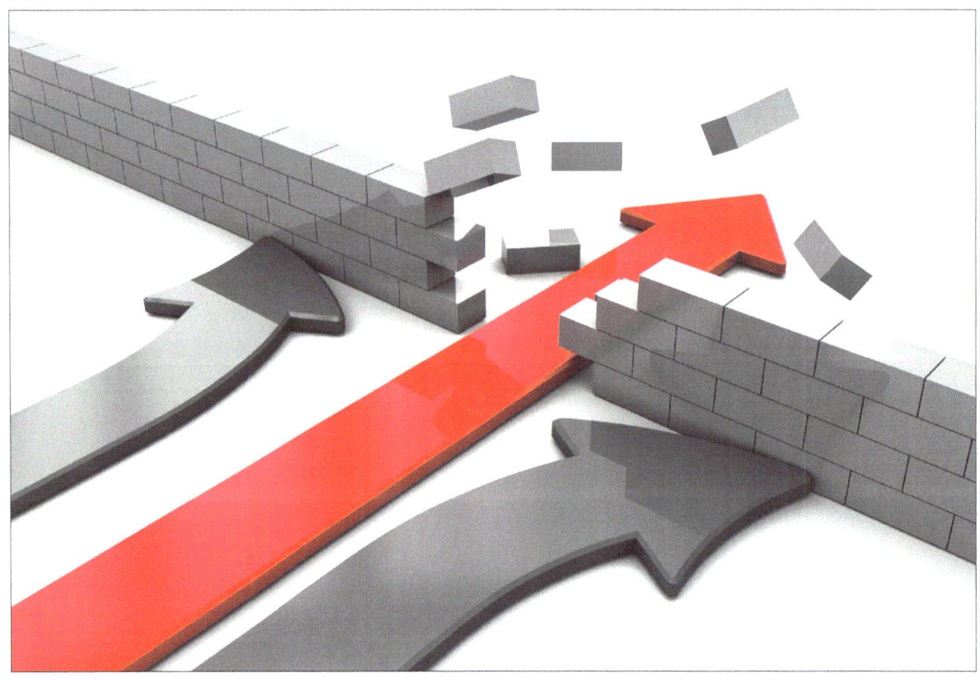

Shutterstock

Don't give up too soon. There will be a period of time when nothing seems to be happening. It is discouraging, and many people impulsively give up at this point. Those who, at the end of the day, achieve great things are those who keep plugging away, even when it seems like they aren't making progress. If you get tired, learn to rest, not to quit.

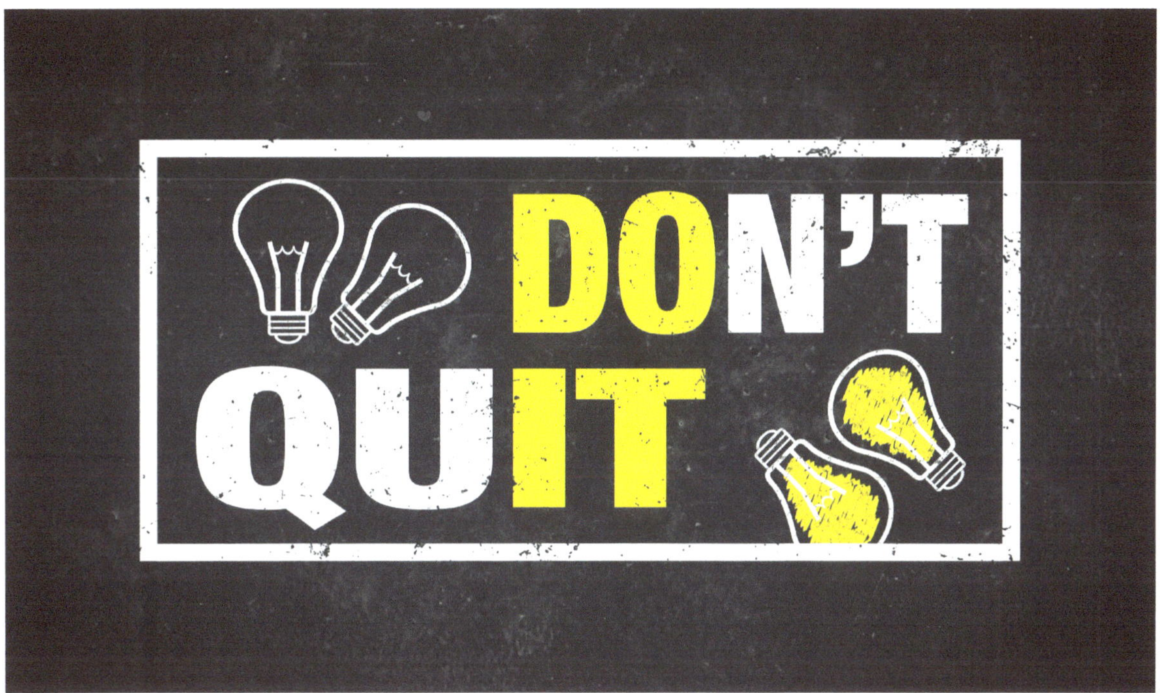

Shutterstock

EVERY DIFFICULTY IS AN OPPORTUNITY IN DISGUISE

Dreams are fragile things. When you are in the beginning stages of creating a life dream goal, you are very exposed. When you have a big goal, you need to be confident so you can attack it head on. You don't need permission to pursue your dream. So, keep it to yourself for a while. Protect it and keep the naysayers at bay.

Pretend you are getting paid, even if you aren't. Very often, when we pursue dreams, we feel a little foolish because there is no money in sight. Don't let that stop you. No one who ever achieved anything great started by making six-figures at it from the get-go. Countless great achievements started with an idea—an unpaid idea. Then there is faith in that idea, followed by hard work and eventual success. Believe in your idea and believe that the time you spend today working toward your goal will be paid for in the future.

There is no career or goal for which you can't find some "expert" who will tell you that what you are trying to do is impossible. If I could outlaw anything on the internet, it would be the thousands of articles where self-proclaimed experts tell people that what they want to do is absurdly hard and to keep your expectations very low. I shudder to think how many great writers, musicians, and leaders the world will never see because someone told them that what they are trying to do is "impossible" or that only one percent of people can achieve that goal. Ignore those people and let them live in mediocrity. If you wish to achieve big dreams, go for it! People don't decide whether your goals will be achieved. Only you do.

Just do it! Don't wait for motivation to strike, or that thing you want to do may never get done. Rather than waiting until you feel like doing it, the magic is to start doing it and then see how you feel.

There is a big distinction between taking inspired action in the course than exerting huge amounts of effort to force yourself into action with push and shove. Approach even the smallest of tasks with a viewpoint of service, love, care, and enjoyment, and you will be surprised at how effortlessly things will begin to unfold before your eyes. Better still, at the end of the day, you will feel empowered rather than drained.

Don't feel you have to go it alone. People are naturally social creatures, but many of us have been conditioned to avoid situations where we have to reveal our true feelings, be open-hearted, and ask for help. It's absolutely okay to reach out to others and ask them for advice, hands-on help, or even just moral support—and the more that you have the courage to do so, the more you will inspire others around you to do the same.

I have personally found that the benefits of letting other people know about my goals has been greater than the downsides—as long as I chose the right people to tell. By sharing goals, reaching out for assistance, and asking people for support, I not only learned how to do it more effectively, but I gained a support team that could help me in achieving the wonderful goals I set.

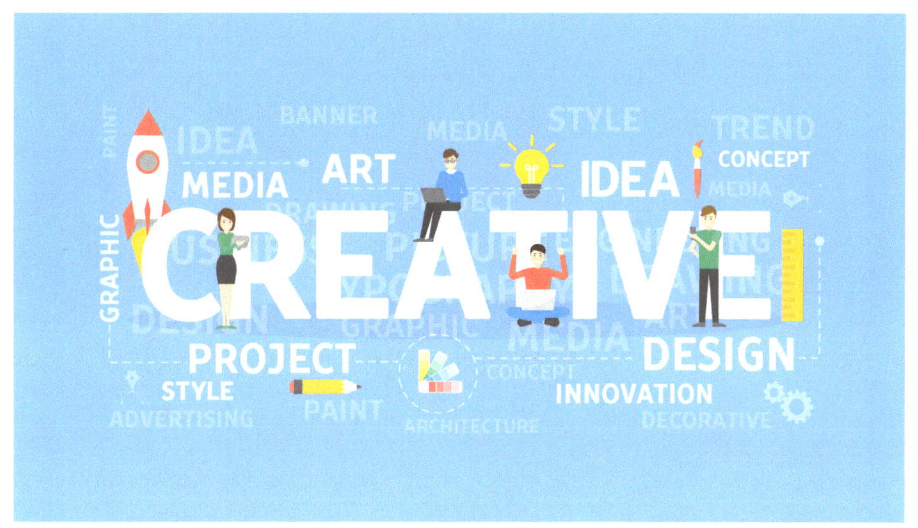

Shutterstock

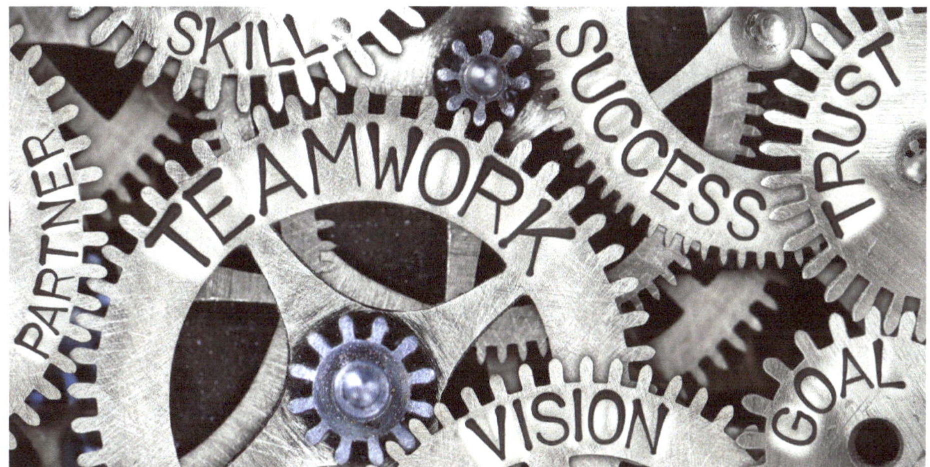

Shutterstock

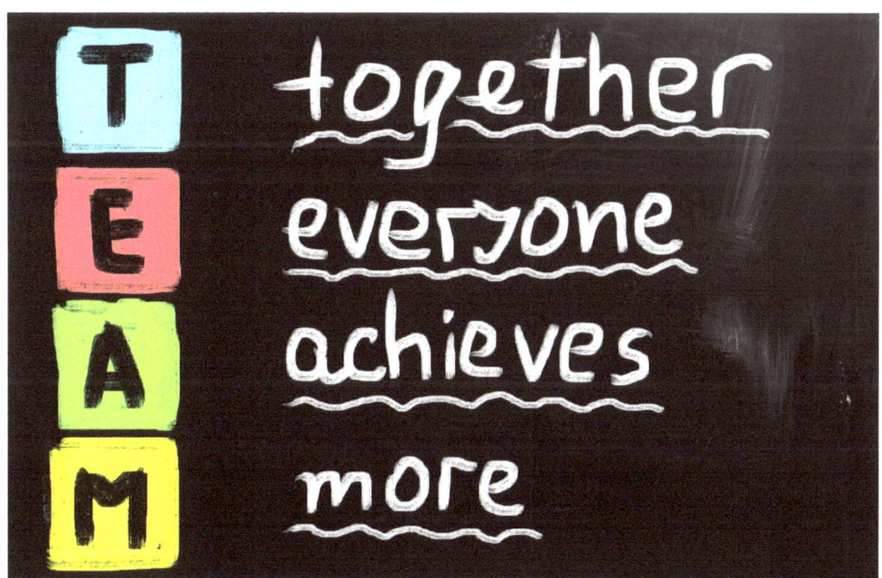

Shutterstock

Chapter 11

Cre8ives As Entrepreneurs

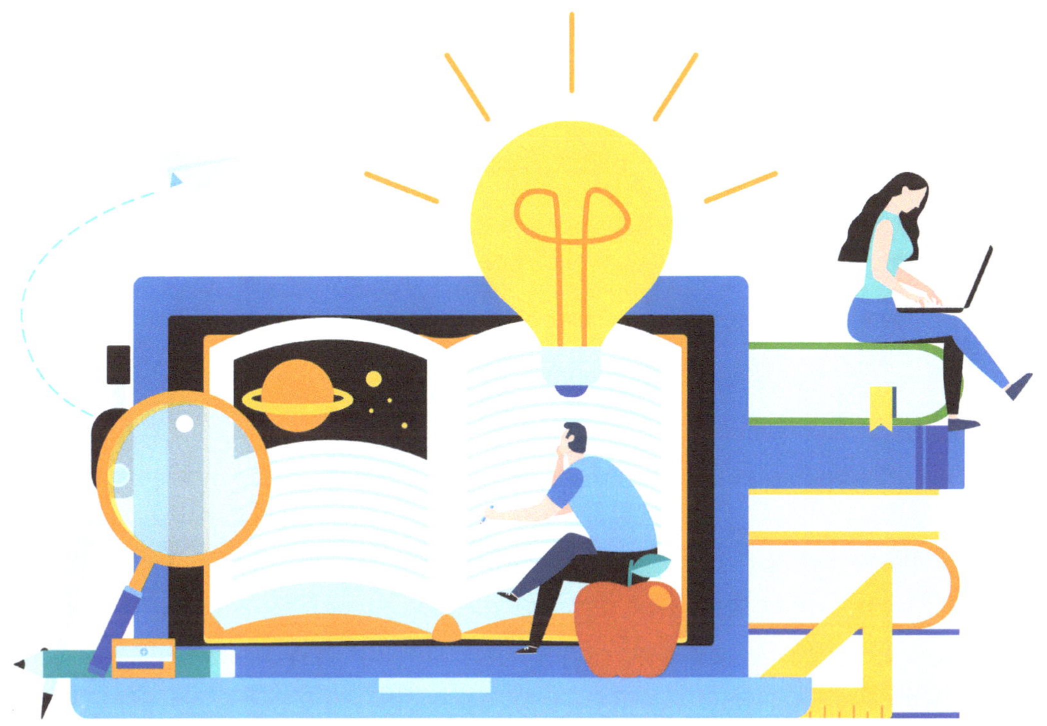

Shutterstock

The entrepreneurial spirit and business strategies can help you develop the talent and dream life you love and create a plan for growth to succeed as a business. The emphasis of this chapter is placed on the development of your entrepreneurial spirit, business techniques, and small business management skills.

"Artists are by nature entrepreneurs; they're just not called that. They have the ability to visualize something that doesn't exist, to look at a canvas and see a painting. Entrepreneurs do that." –Bill Strickland, *Founder of the Manchester Craftsmen's Guild*

The word entrepreneur is from the old French word *entreprendre*, to undertake. The Webster Dictionary definition today is, "*one who organizes, manages, and assumes the risks of a business or enterprise.*" The traditional entrepreneur is motivated by wealth and or attaining power by heading up their own business. They love the business of business. A creative entrepreneur may have the same allure as a traditionalist, but many creatives are looking to build a business to gain freedom or control over their lives, to give rise to a business that revolves around what they are good at or enjoy doing most: producing art.

For the creative entrepreneur it's about consequence of life or pursuing your passion. Any time commerce money comes into play, most entrepreneurial creatives are not in business to grow their hometown enterprise into a public company traded on the New York Stock Exchange. They simply want to do what they love and have a contented livelihood.

❖ An entrepreneur is a true "innovator," one who recognizes opportunity and organizes resources to take advantage of the opportunity. Entrepreneurship is about hard work, reducing risk, and promoting a simple solution. Entrepreneurs are risk reducers and leave nothing to chance.

❖ Developing the entrepreneurial spirit and comprehension of business strategies can help the artist develop the work they love and create a plan for growth to succeed as a business. Emerging, mid-career, and seasoned artists alike can take control of their own careers by becoming their own gallery dealer, museum curator, business manager, and strategic marketer. As they successfully develop their art marketing capabilities and hone their business skills, artists who participate in business career training more often than not renew their art direction and build their confidence at the same time. The end work of art is a productive, satisfying, and sustainable career-life as an artist.

❖ Gain an understanding how to take your talent as a cre8ive and developing this talent offering into a viable business offering for your target audience needs. This includes development of your cre8ives offering statement.

❖ Understanding the basic overview of the business plan including the executive summary, company description, strategic focus and plan, marketing and product objectives, marketing program, implementation plan, evaluation and control, and financial projections.

❖ Business financing includes sources of capital for financing a business, relationship between risk and reward, debt and equity financing, and personal credit. Learn how to find capital, including grant writing and government funding sources.

❖ Business sustainability—develop the ability to keep the business growing and expanding through ongoing marketing and operational planning. This will also teach the dangers of success and focus on long term viability.

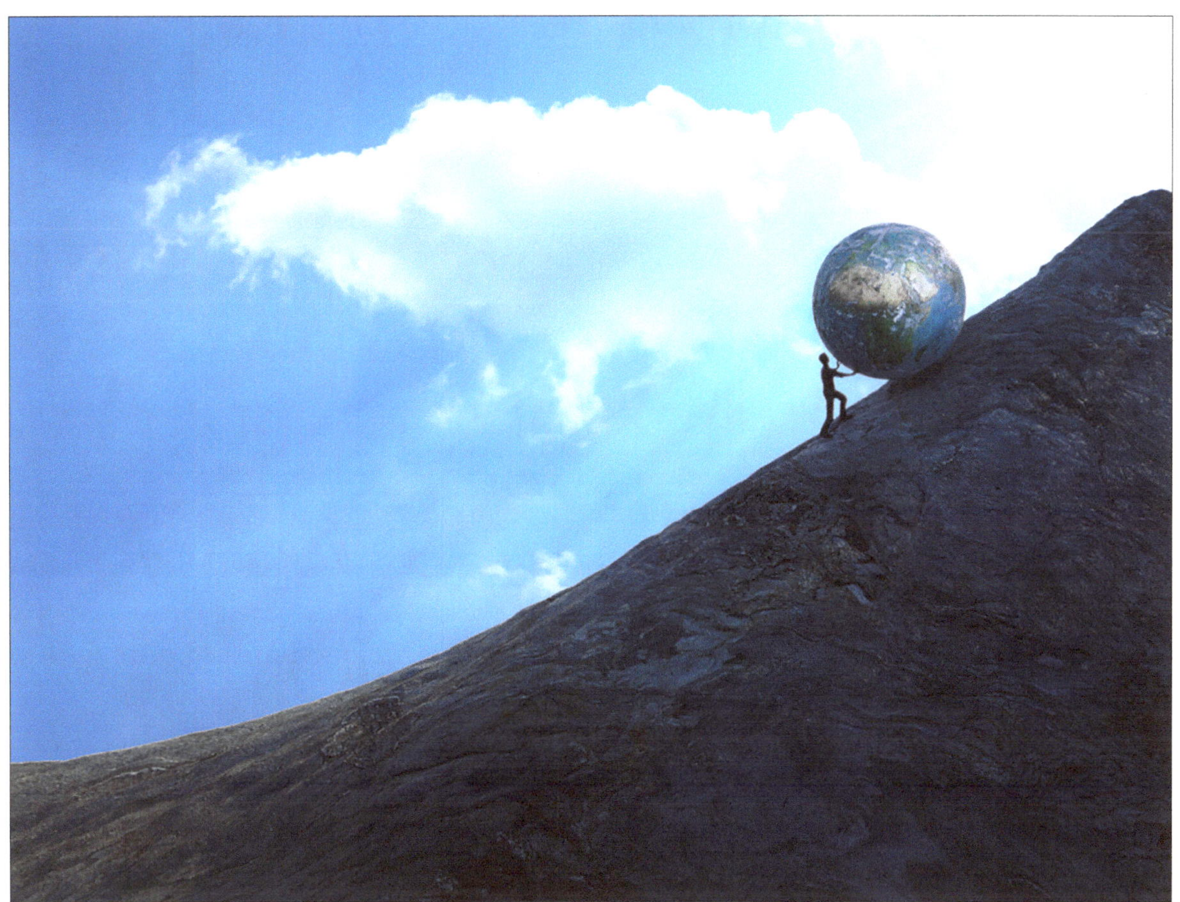

Shutterstock

Business cycle summary

DEFINED

- Those activities which should occur before getting into business.

- Generally, no income in this stage, therefore, expenses should be of a non-recurring nature—that is, no fixed overhead.

- Ideally, other sources of income are available.

FREQUENT KEYS TO SURVIVAL

- Taking enough time; examining one's own strengths and weaknesses.

- Examining possibility of supplementing own experience and talents with others, such as a working partner.

COMMON CAUSES OF DISASTER

- Jumping in too soon.

- Getting stuck with an overhead before there is income.

- Making premature commitments to partners and suppliers.

- Giving equity to advisers.

FINANCE

- Funds usually from would-be owner and immediate family and friends.

- If bank support, usually personally guaranteed or fully collateralized.

- No income, all expenses.

- A cash "hog" and difficult to predict costs.

- Preliminary searching for future funds—banks, government partners, individual backers.

SUPPLY AND TECHNOLOGY

- Generally, no locked-in source of supply.

- Rather subcontract short experimental-type product runs.

- Sample only produced.

- Need to experiment and adapt.

- Don't get wedded to product or concept if changes are indicated.

MARKET

- Few "sales," rather free samples. Testing, feedback.

- Market tends to indicate more interest and enthusiasm than is really meant. Discount heavily statements of future intent.

MANAGEMENT/PEOPLE

- Possibility of working partner—must complement areas of weakness.

- Danger of talking to "outsiders" because of entrepreneur's insecurity—overly jealous of personal ideas and plans.

The Power of Teams
Using Teams to Meet Today's Challenges

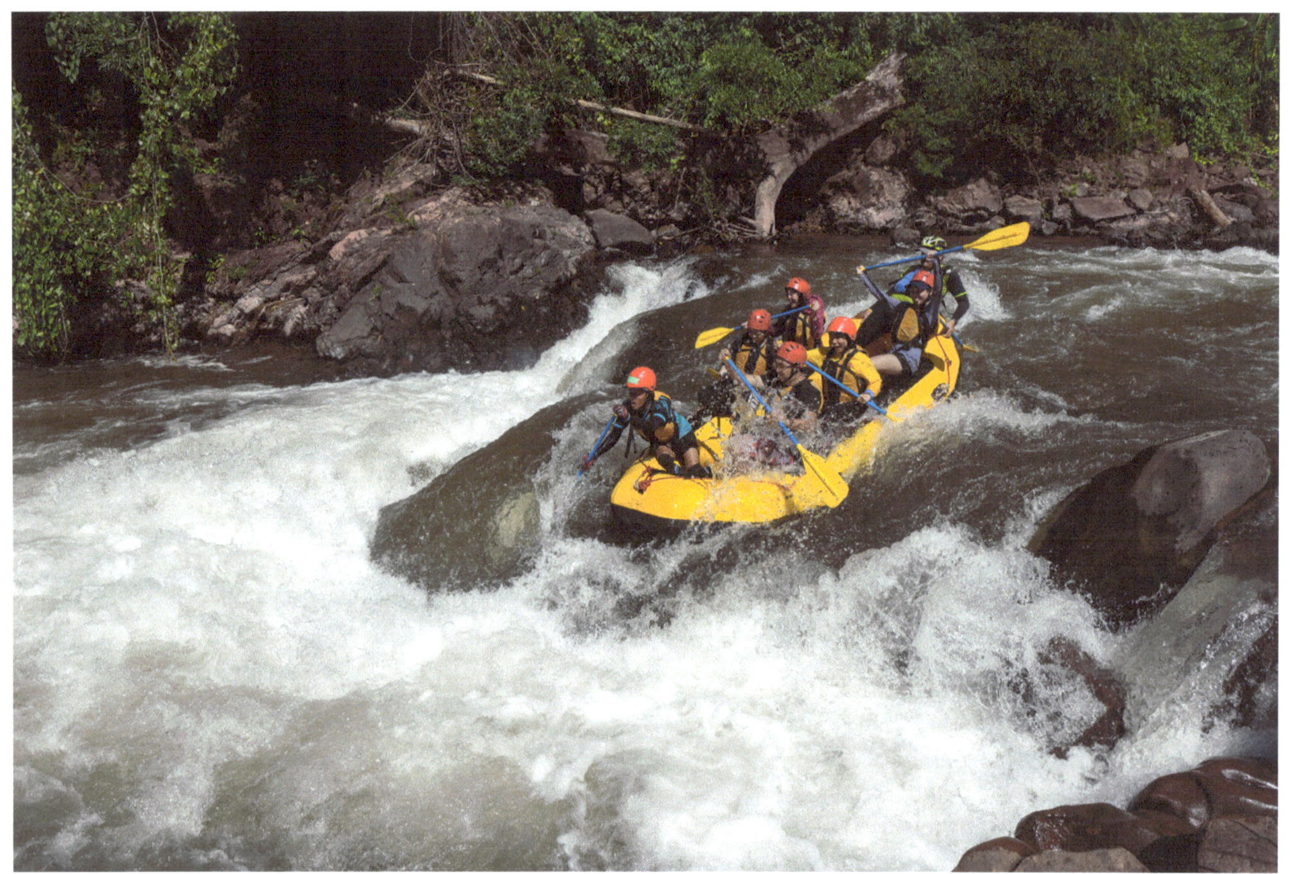

Shutterstock

The Dynamic, Productive Team

- ➢ The task is complex

- ➢ Creativity is needed

- ➢ The path forward is unclear

- ➢ More efficient use of resources is required

- ➢ Fast learning is necessary

- ➢ High commitment is desirable

- ➢ Cooperation is essential to implementation

- ➢ Members have a stake in the outcome

- ➢ The task or process involved is cross-functional

- ➢ No individual has sufficient knowledge to solve the problem

Teams Have the Ability to:

- ➢ Reduce lead times

- ➢ Decrease cycle time

- ➢ Cut service errors

- ➢ Manage processes

- ➢ Perform daily work

- ➢ Increase the rate of transactions

- ➢ Develop new products and services

- ➢ Operate organizational units

- ➢ Redesign systems

- ➢ Understand customer needs

- ➢ Write business plans

Ten Ingredients for a Successful Team

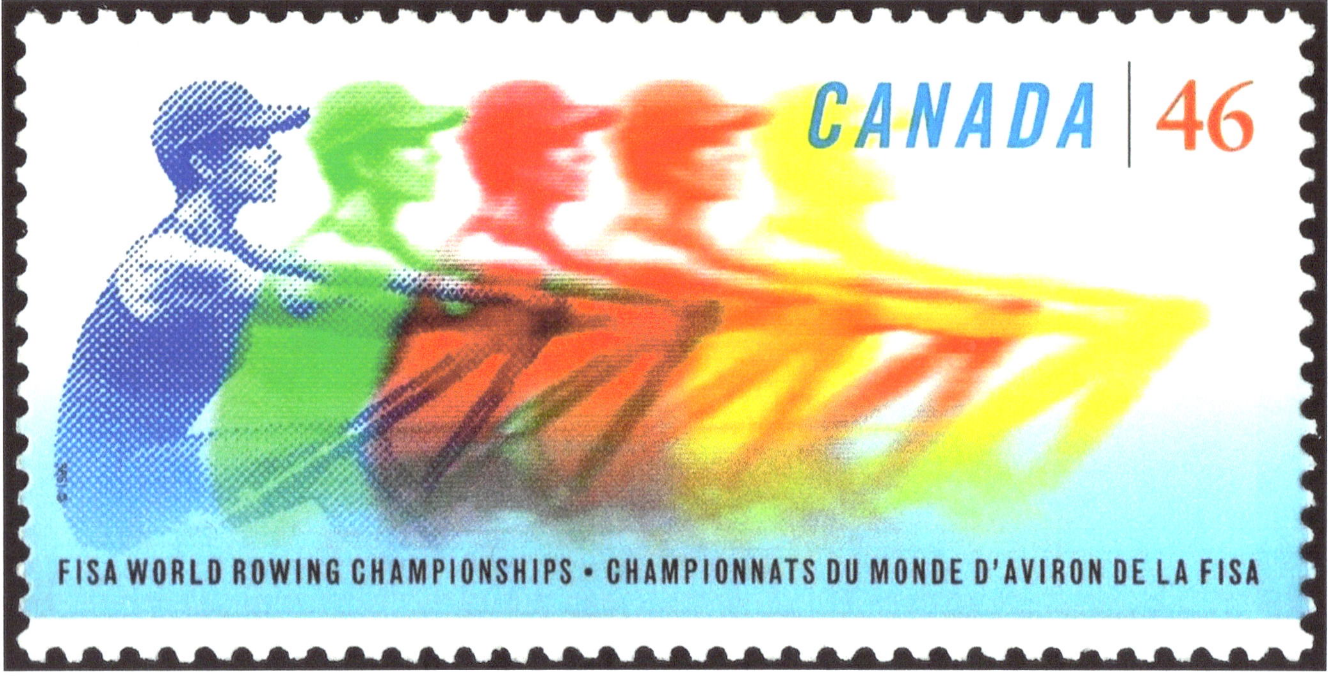

CANADIAN POSTAGE STAMP

> Clarity in team goals

> A plan for improvement

> Clearly defined goals

> Clear communication

> Beneficial team behavior

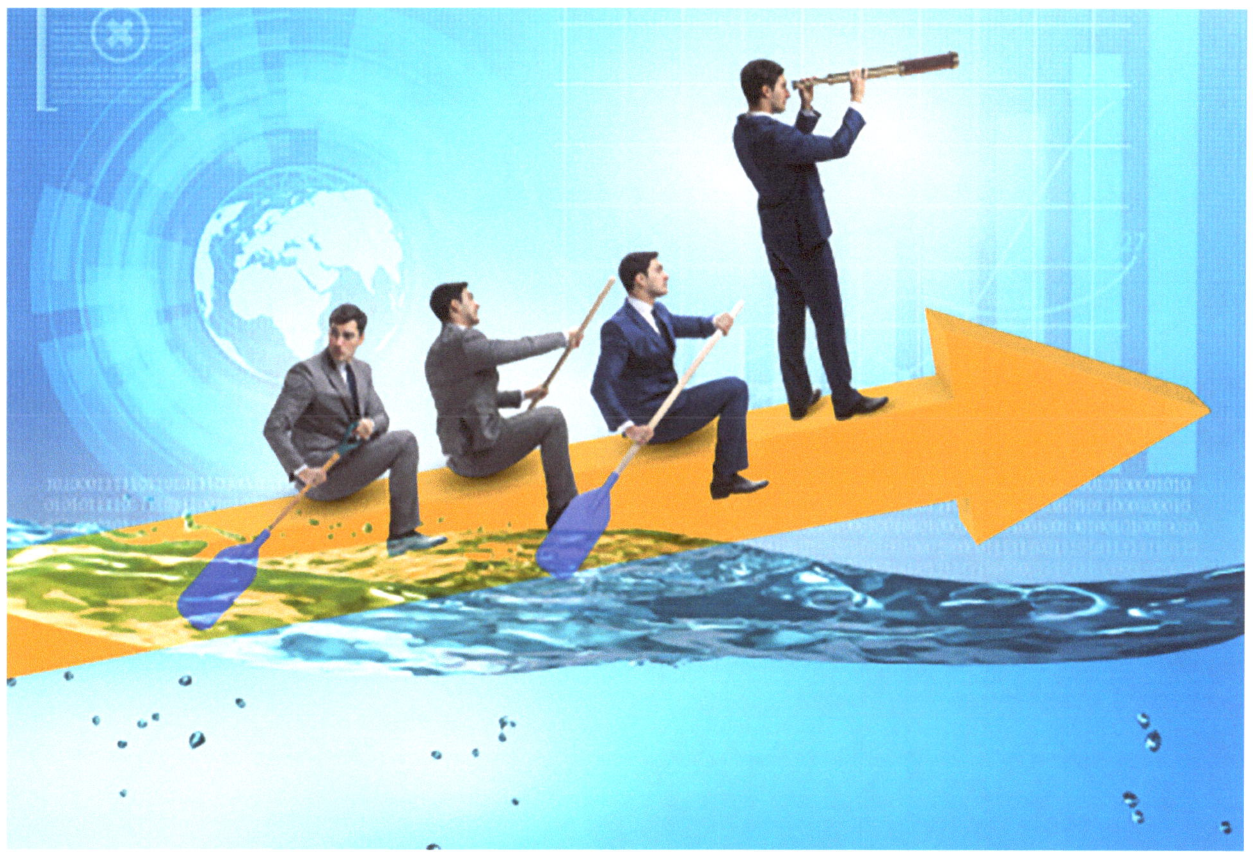

Shutterstock

➢ Well-defined decision procedures

➢ Balanced participation

➢ Established ground rules

➢ Awareness of the group process

➢ Use of the scientific approach

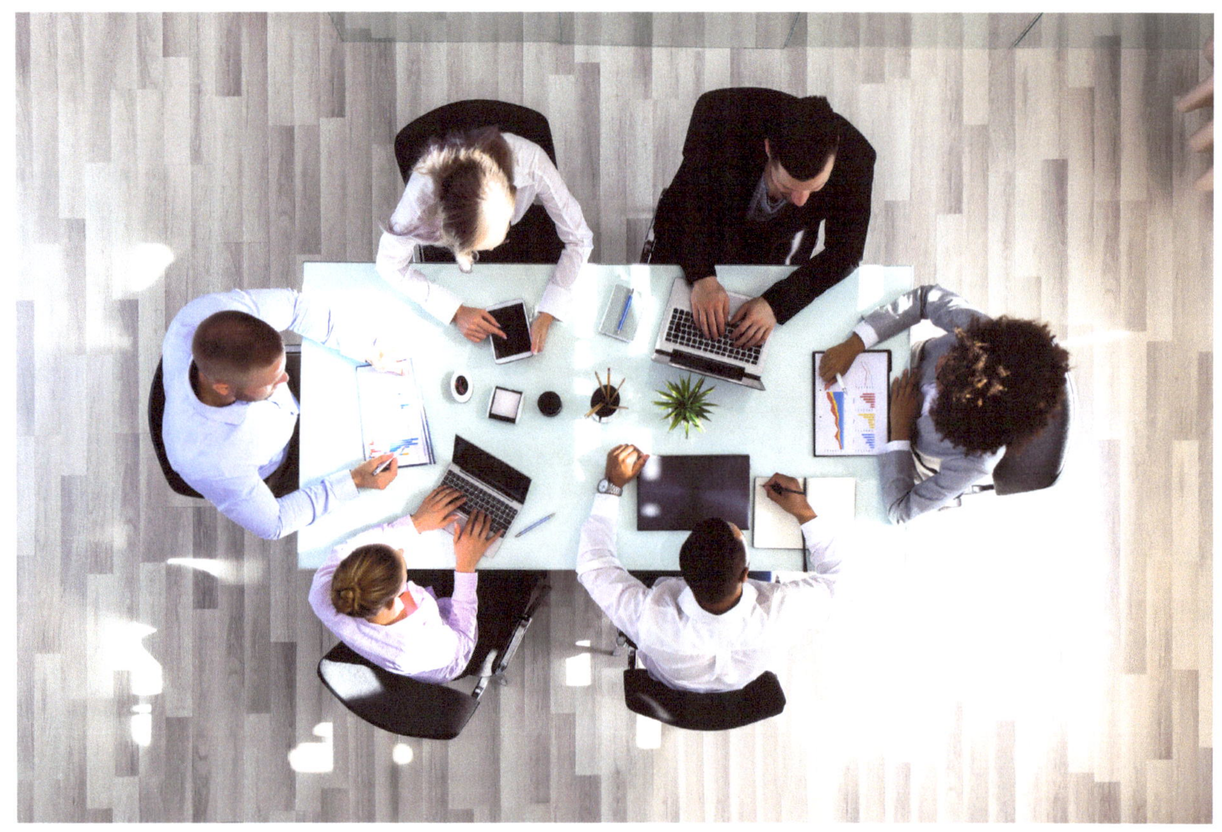

Shutterstock

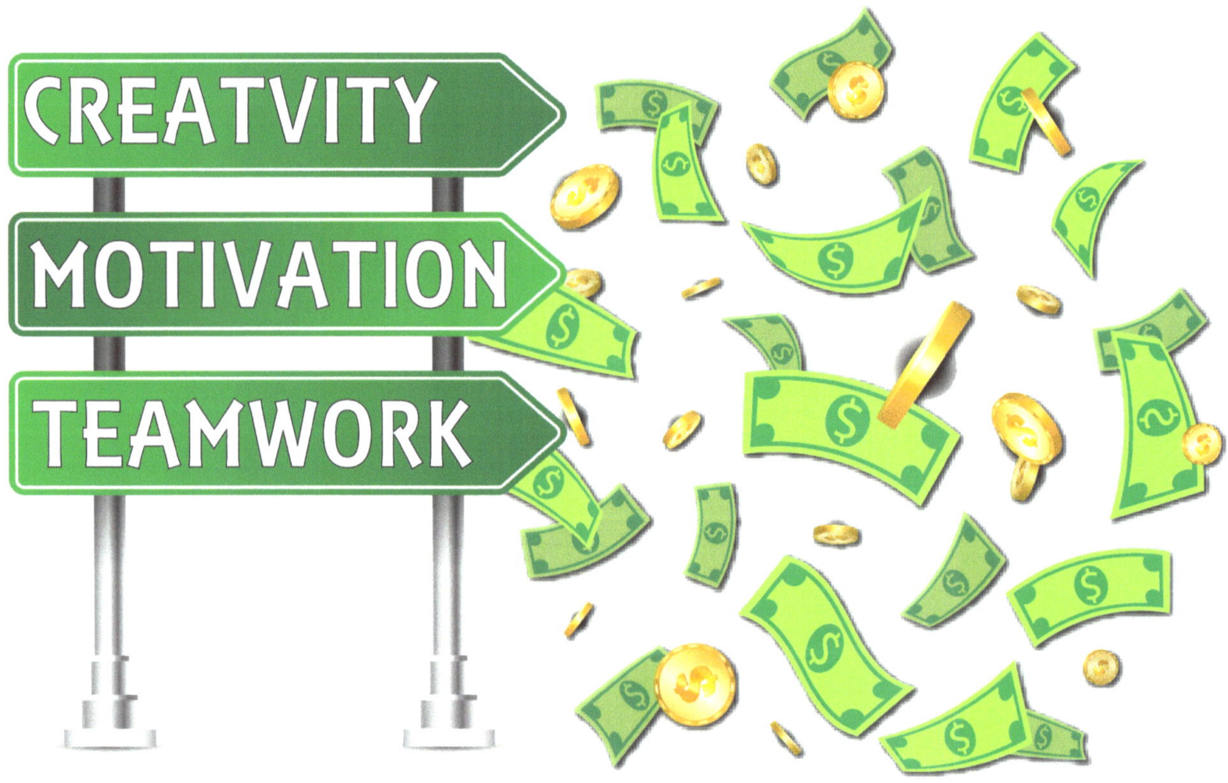

Nancy McKarney

Chapter 12
Entrepreneurs Are Go-Getters

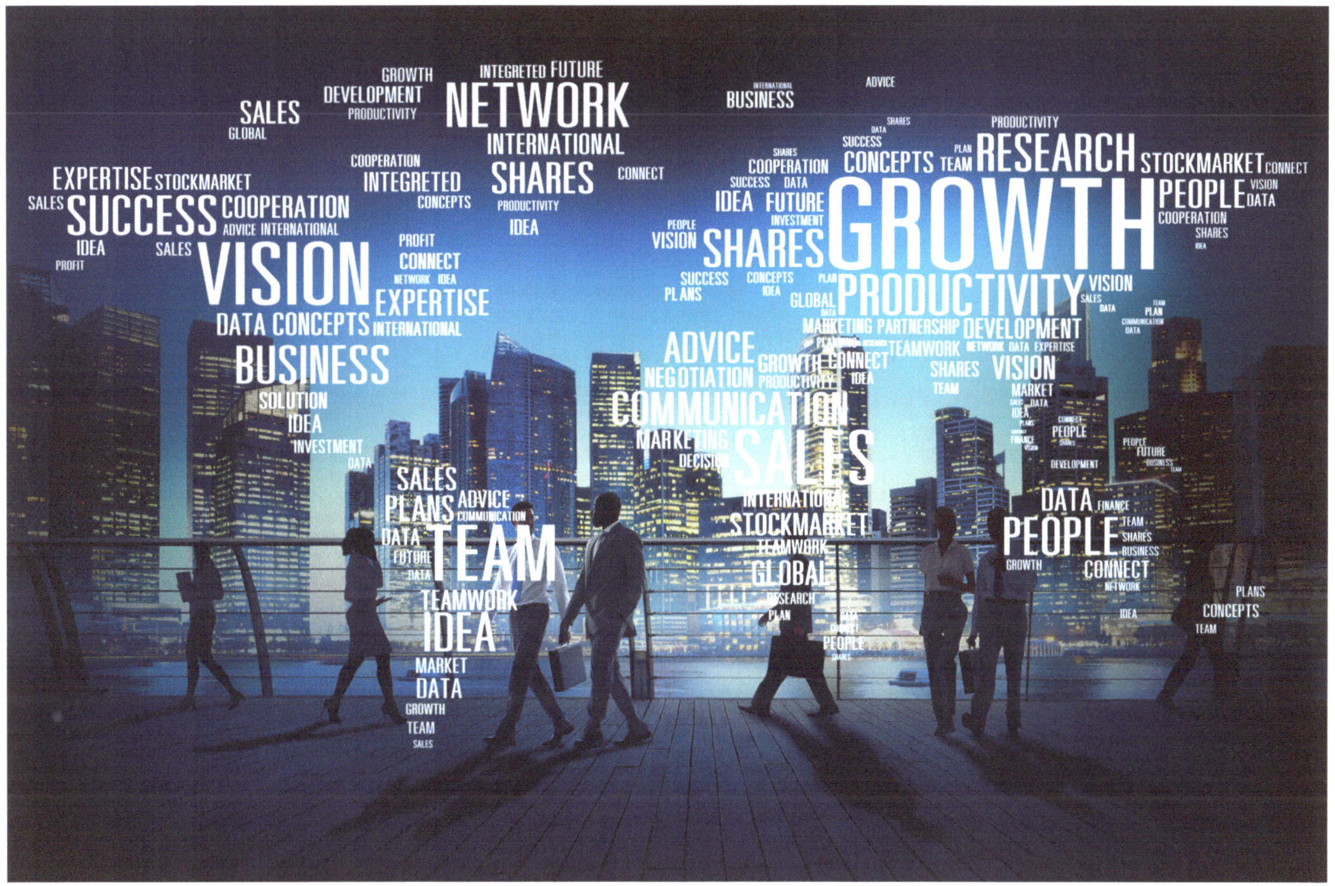

Shutterstock

Once upon a time, I had a front-row seat and witnessed, up close and personal, the childhood *dream come true* of an adult entrepreneurial artist, creating great works of art as he painted at the easel in his studio and on location Plein Air paintings. Using motion-picture technology, I chronicled Thomas Kinkade, the self-proclaimed "Painter of Light"®.

Love his art or dislike it, the fact is Thomas Kinkade was to art what Henry Ford was to automobiles. His studio paintings focused on sentimental depictions of babbling brooks, rural churches, dreamscape idyllic cottages, wilderness cabins, Victorian-style homes, gardens, and historical street scenes.

For seven and half years, I worked closely with Thom as I called him. I was his television director and producer. One fellow colleague, Eric Kuskey, wrote in his book, *BILLION DOLLAR PAINTER The Triumph and Tragedy of THOMAS KINKADE, Painter of Light.*

> Terry Sheppard had been promised the keys to the kingdom by Thom. He was the one guy who was always there for Thom and who had an insight into his life like almost no one else had. Terry was the staple in his posse; he chronicled every minute of Thom's life for posterity. There was a time when Thom didn't go anywhere without Terry. It seemed like he wouldn't go the grocery store without Terry there with his omnipresent camera, capturing the Painter of Light in his ordinary and extraordinary moments. In that sense, he was the most important person in Thom's life.

Thom grew up in a single-parent home with his younger brother and older sister. They were very impoverished. His mother sometimes worked two jobs to support the family. It was a happy home. When Thom was young, he had a childhood dream of being an artist. He began to set his course to fulfill that dream. He was very focused and knew what he wanted to be at a very early age. As he grew older, he knew where he was going, and if it took seven days a week, he was going to get there.

I learned from Thom's mother Mary Ann that he started from scratch, stretching his own canvases. As he grew older, he studied every famous artist and went deep into their lives. He wanted to be like them. He developed his talent. He worked at it. He had the ability to work long and hard and stick with it. Talent is talent, but you have to work at it. When he was in high school, he became known as the artist. He had a willingness to get out and promote himself and his art.

Thom and his wife Nanette established their entrepreneurial enterprise, Lightpost Publishing, in their childhood hometown, Placerville, California. Thom was a complete outsider to the mainstream high art world, as defined by museums and New York galleries. Thomas Kinkade, the "Painter of Light"® became a modestly successful artist, selling his original paintings and print reproductions of country cottages, village street scenes, gardens, and streams. Kinkade agreed with a new business partner, Ken Raasch, to morph his home-grown Lightpost Publishing into a publicly traded corporation under the banner of Media Arts Group, Inc. The financial business values and strategy put in place at the beginning of the public corporation were shrewd and calculating.

The idealistic images Thom painted truly touched people's emotions. The ache of the heart in a world of shadows and despair set the stage for the unprecedented popularity of his paintings. The "Painter of Light"® was one of the most successful and misunderstood artists who ever lived. His art was loved by the public but derided by the art establishment. Art critics often called his homey heart-warming paintings, "schmaltz and kitsch."

During the 1980s, New York art dealers, critics, and curators moved artists from first recognition to phenomenal commercial success in abundance. In our day, many art dealers are like dealers in exotic collectibles and luxury cars or any nonessential good, for that matter.

Across America and around the world at this time, scores of artists maintained they had the benefit of the act of artistic expression, creating work that brought them pleasure, while enriching the lives of the general population and growing rich in the course of action.

While art aficionados championed Warhol's Soup Cans and Lichtenstein's comic-book with art tributes, many despised and some even hated Kinkade's art. When I asked Thom once to comment on the critics' disdain for his artistic works he replied, *"What I paint is foundational, home, family, and peacefulness."* Thom laughed all the way to the bank.

Thomas Kinkade sold millions of his inspiring paintings on mass-produced paper and canvas lithographs. An adoring group of Christians and traditional art collectors and distributors were his target market. It is estimated that today one of every twenty households in America has one of his reproduced paintings hanging on their living room walls. His idealistic images truly touched people's hearts. His paintings take the viewer to a place they would like to be. I call his paintings the three-second vacation.

Thom turned his childhood passion to be an artist into a multibillion-dollar empire. It was an astonishing journey as my friend's success fostered temptation and greed, the perils of fame and fortune. With more than four billion dollars in reproduced art retail sales and licensing royalties, Kinkade became the most financially successful artist-painter who ever lived. He would sell one million dollars' worth of his art painting prints on QVC in an hour. In 2002, CBS television's news magazine, *60 Minutes*, was ranked sixth on TV Guide's list of the fifty greatest TV shows of all time. The *New York Times* called *60 Minutes*, "one of the most esteemed news magazines on American television." *60 Minutes* news anchor and host Morley Safer did a *60 Minutes* interview with Thomas Kinkade, showcasing his art. The show also included how the "Painter of Light's" original artworks were reproduced on paper and canvas. Morley wrapped up the on-air Kinkade profile with this declaration, *"Thomas Kinkade sold more canvas that any other painter in history. More than Picasso, Rembrandt, Monet, Manet, Renoir, and Van Gogh combined. He is America's, and the world's, most collected artist."*

Over a five-year period, I directed and produced *"An American Artist: The Thomas Kinkade Life Story."* It was filmed in locations across the United States, Europe, and Central America. The final edited documentary with no commercial breaks premiered on national television as a PBS One-Hour Special in 2003. It went on to become a PBS Television Network

"Pledge Break Special." According to PBS, a "Pledge Break Special" is broadcast numerous times over many months following the premiere to an estimated audience of 98 million PBS viewers.

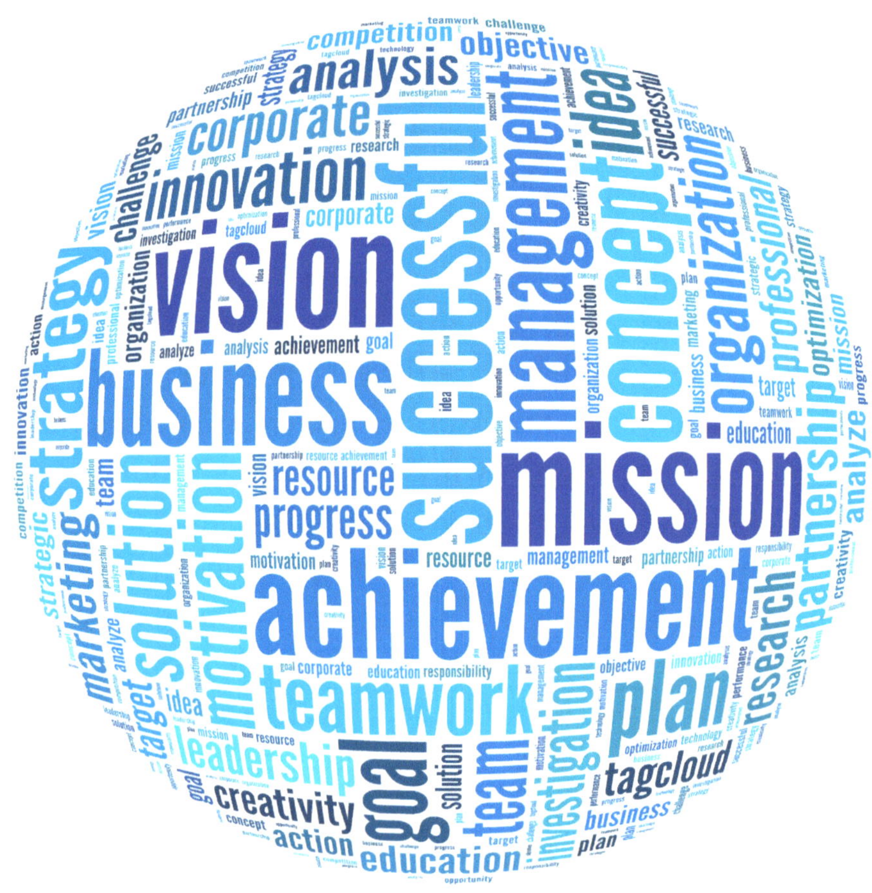

Shutterstock

Propelling Business and Life Success

While less than 15% of the United States workforce is self-employed, these entrepreneurs represent over 66% of our millionaires. Why? Are they smarter? More talented? No! Entrepreneurs simply focus on opportunities and take action. They don't over-analyze. Furthermore, they take 100% responsibility for their results—no excuses and no blaming.

Successful entrepreneurs set their goals. They take action, monitor, and own the results, and make adjustments as they go with goals, action, feedback, adjustments, and more action. Their mode of operation of "Ready, Aim, Go—Adjust Aim, Go, Go, Go." The emphasis is on doing, not the preparing.

Nothing good happens until you act, start moving. Action always eclipses inaction. By taking action, entrepreneurs learn from the marketplace and make real-time corrections based on current facts, not speculation.

On the other hand, others focus on obstacles and analysis. They focus on "what can go wrong." They are ruled by fear, comfort zones, and excuses. Their mode of operation is "Ready, Ready, Plan, Plan, and more Plan." They don't execute or take action. They want to know all the answers before they start. They want to eliminate all risks and unknowns. They want guarantees. This is unrealistic and will only guarantee a lack of success. Deadly analysis-paralysis take over.

Where are you stalling in life? What are you putting off because of fear or imperfect information? What project do you have on hold? What dream is on delay? The entrepreneur's solution would be to start now, wherever you are, with whatever you got. Take some action and learn in the process.

"Don't wait. The time will never be just right."
—Napoleon Hill

Strategic Planning

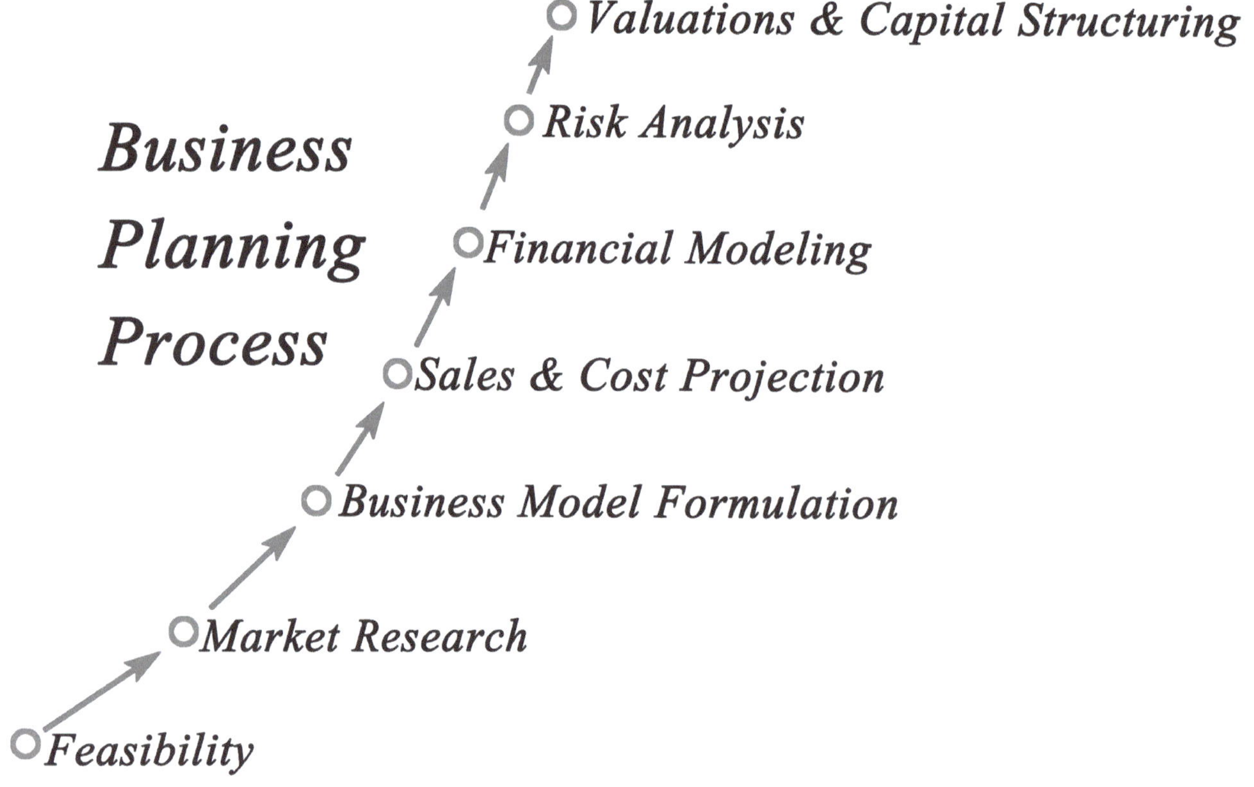

Shutterstock

Financing of Company Development

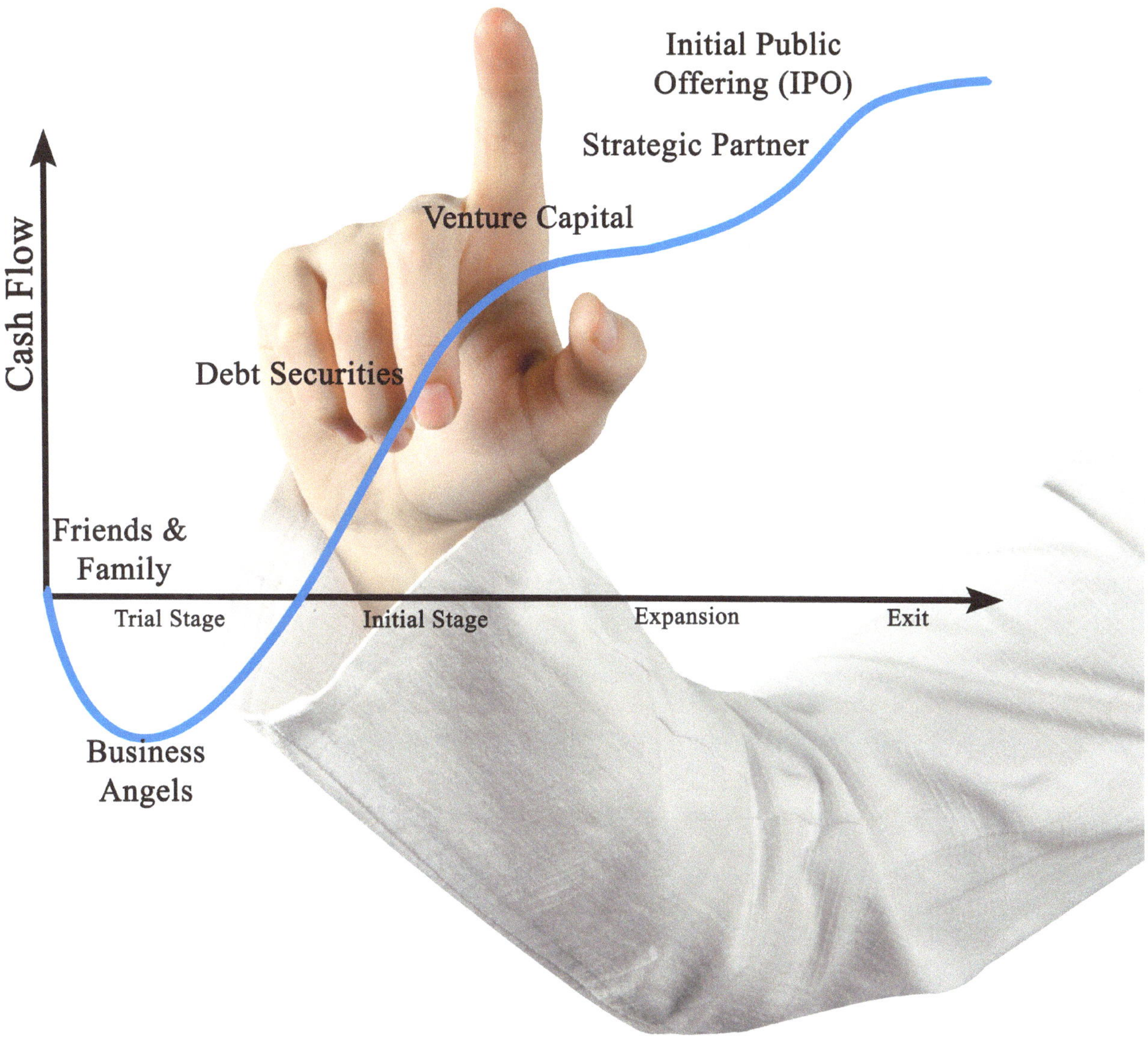

Shutterstock

❖ **Phases**

- ✓ Identify the stages of growth (seed capital)

- ✓ Expansion phase requires capital for a proven concept

- ✓ Mezzanine/bridge financing

❖ **Bootstrapping**

- ✓ Techniques for getting by on as few resources as possible and using other people's resources whenever feasible:
  - Begging
  - Borrowing
  - Leasing

❖ **Bootstrapping tips**

- ✓ Hire as few employees as possible

- ✓ Lease or share everything

- ✓ Use other people's money

- ✓ Remain ethical

Entrepreneur Resources

❖ **Startup capital structure includes**

   ✓ Savings

   ✓ Credit cards

   ✓ Mortgages

   ✓ Stock market accounts

   ✓ Vendor credit

   ✓ Customer financing

   ✓ Loans

Financing with Equity

❖ **Equity from friends and family**

   ✓ The most expensive long-term funding

   ✓ The entrepreneur is more likely to lose control of the business

❖ **Private investors—Angels**

   ✓ Angels are informal risk capital sources

   ✓ Funding is between $10K—$500K

✓ Angels are often well-educated entrepreneurs who tend to invest within a short distance from home

✓ Angels take an active role in the company

❖ **Private placement**

✓ Private investments obtained by selling securities in a private corporation/ partnership

✓ SEC Regulation D covers memorandum details

✓ Advantages

- Few prior assets or credit references are needed
- No SEC filing needed for entrepreneurs

✓ Strategic Alliances

- Formal/informal partnerships with other businesses

✓ Small Business Investment Companies (SBIC) privately managed venture capital firms licensed by the Small Business Administration

✓ Grants

✓ Venture Capital Institutes and Network

Financing with Debt

❖ **Commercial banks**

  ✓ Basis of loans

- Character
- Capacity
- Capital
- Collateral
- Condition

❖ **Commercial finance companies**

  ✓ Less regulated than banks

  ✓ High finance charges

  ✓ Factoring

- Receivable financing in which the factor takes ownership of a receivable at a discount and then collects against it

❖ **Small Business Administration loan**

  ✓ Entrepreneur applies for up to $2M loan from their personal bank; BA guarantees that it will repay up to 75% of the loan to the commercial lender should the business default

  ✓ Micro loans exist for companies to use nonprofit community development corporations rather than banks

❖ **State-funded venture capital**

❖ **Incubators**

❖ **Customers and suppliers**

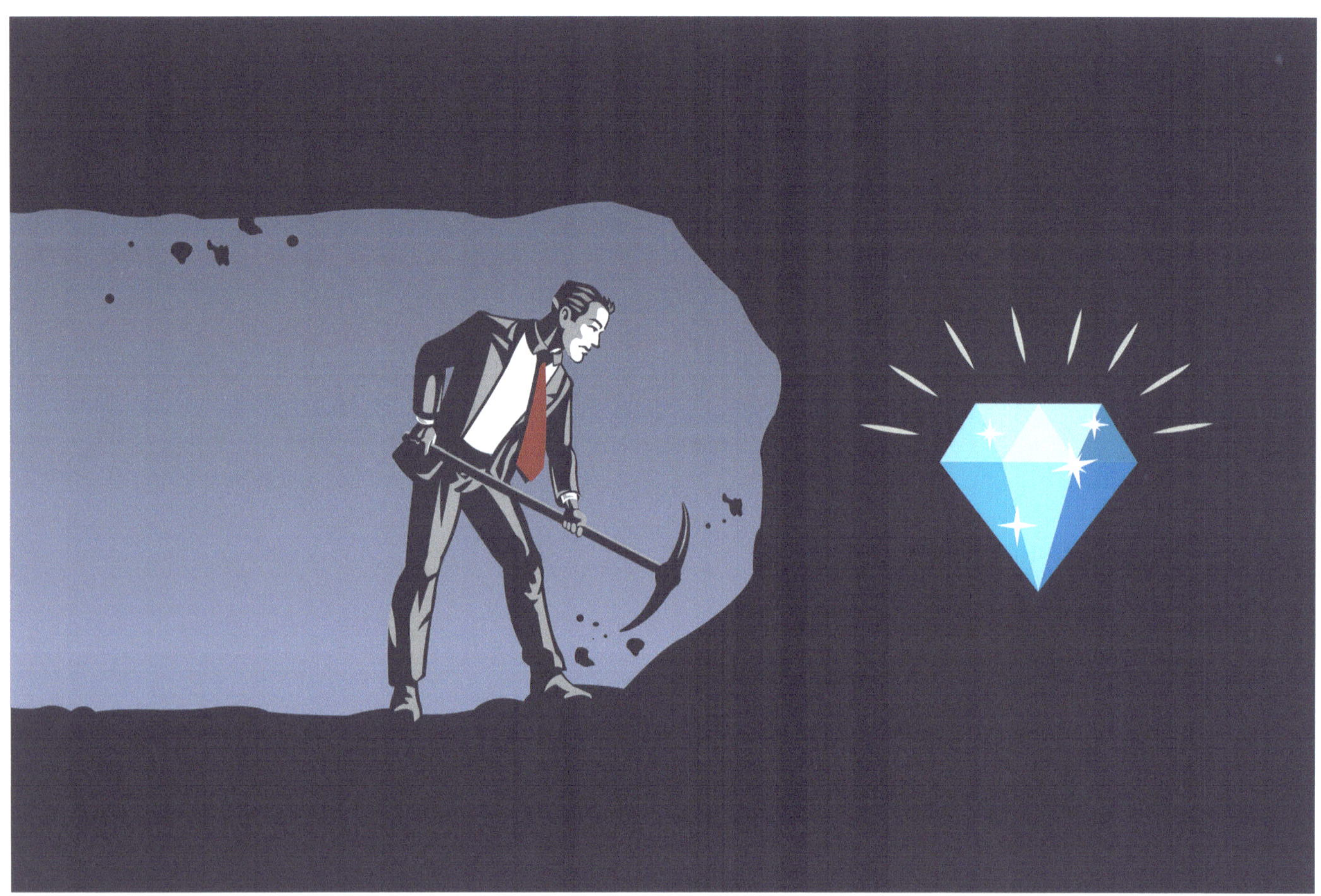

Shutterstock

Chapter 13

Organize Your Business

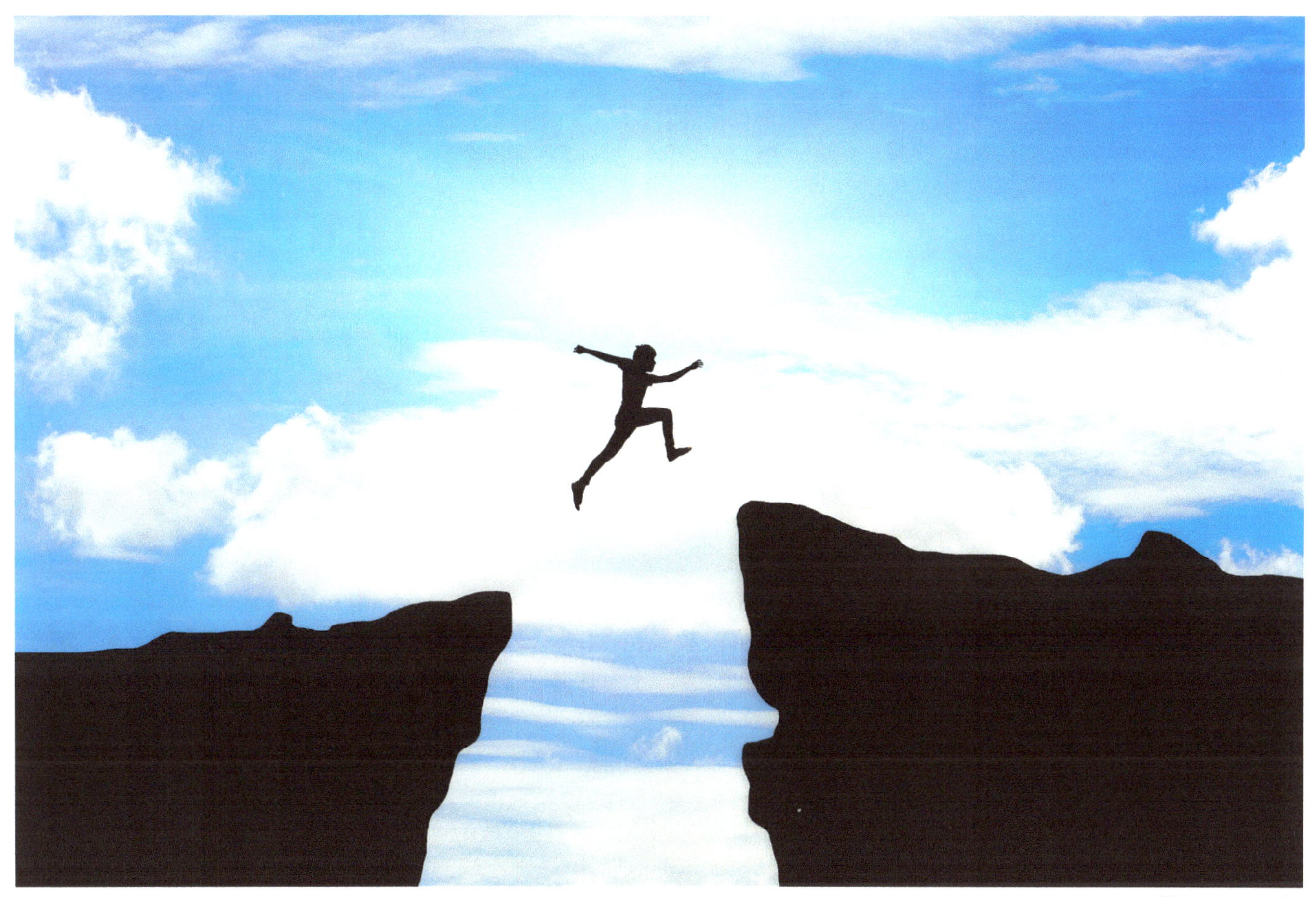

Shutterstock

THE DISTANCE BETWEEN
YOUR DREAMS AND REALITY
IS CALLED ACTION.

Starting the Process with a Presentation

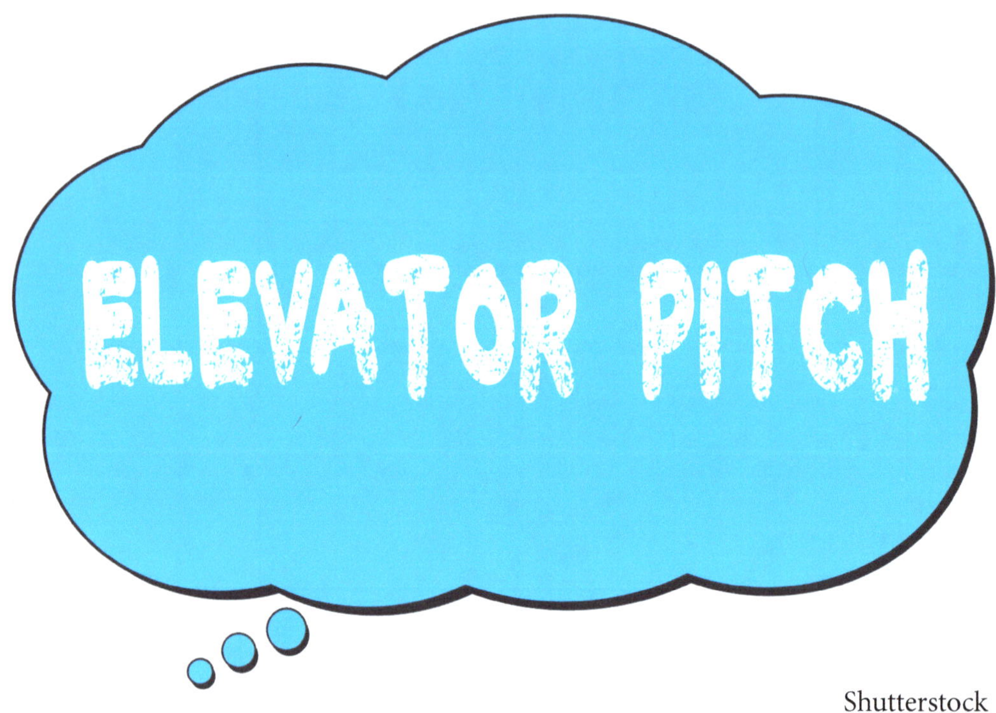

Shutterstock

➢ Prepare a brief statement of the business concept.

➢ Answer the following questions:

   o Why you, why now, and how will you change the world?

   o What need is being served?

   o Can the founding team serve the need?

   o Why is now the right time to launch this venture?

   o What is the venture's competitive advantage?

   o Can this venture make money?

Starting the Process with a Presentation

The Elevator Pitch

Action-Oriented Description

- ✓ Thirty-second presentation of 100 words or less.

- ✓ Designed to sell the idea of the venture to another.

- ✓ Four success factors.

    - o The hook

    - o The purpose

    - o What and where

    - o The delivery

How to Write Your Elevator Pitch

- ✓ **First, the Hook**—something about your service or product that people can take away.

- ✓ Try using an analogy.

- ✓ Different pitches for different audiences.

    - o Investors

    - o Customers

    - o Suppliers

- ✓ **Second, Focus**—on the purpose your service or product serves for the customer.

- ✓ Do not talk skills.

✓ Talk about how you make customers happy.

✓ **Third, the Business Situation**—It's a startup.

✓ What the business is seeking (funding, partners, distributors, etc.).

✓ If it is operating, tell the reader or listener where he or she can buy service or product.

From Feasibility Study

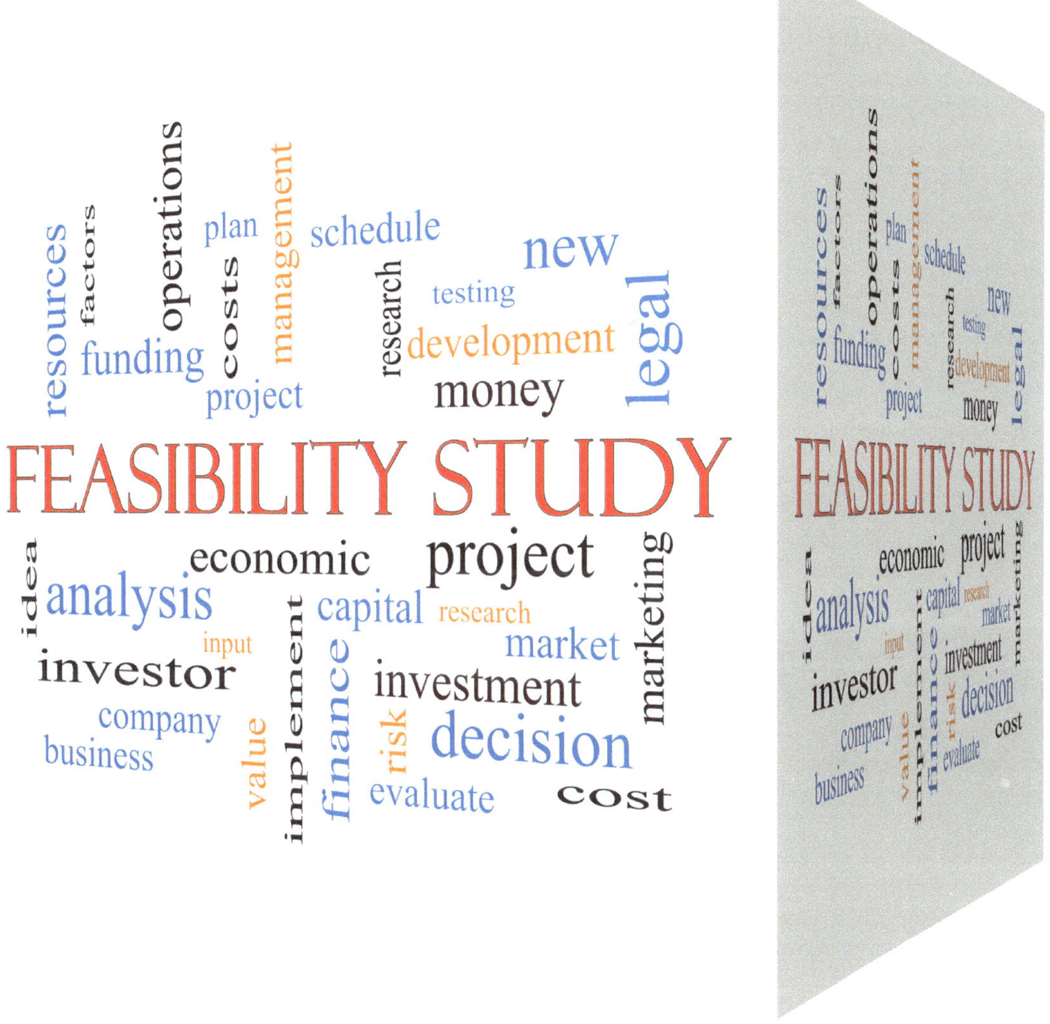

Shutterstock

To Business Plan

Purpose of the business plan

o   Serves as a reality check for the entrepreneur.

o   Is a living guide to the business.

o   Is it a statement of intent for interested third parties?

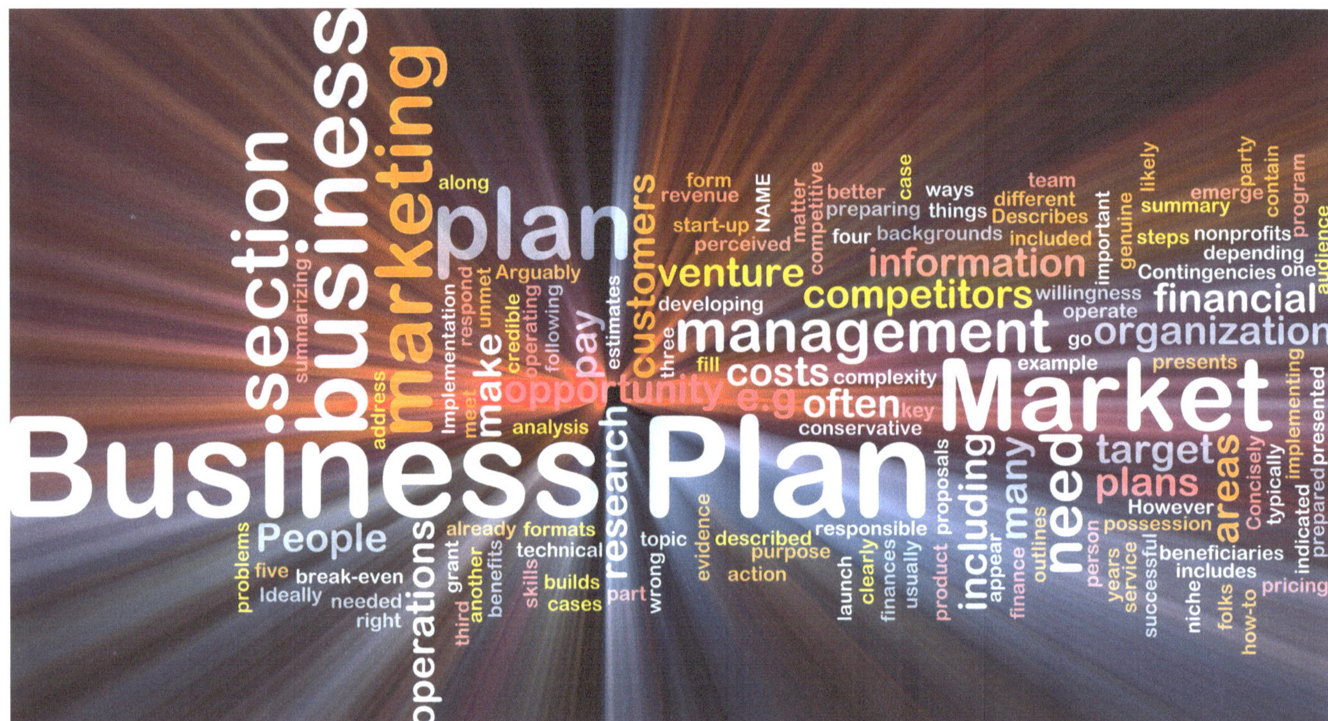

Shutterstock

Fourteen "personal" questions every business plan should answer:

- Where are the founders from?

- Where have they been educated?

- Where have they worked—and for whom?

- What have they accomplished—professionally and personally—in the past?

- What is their reputation within the business community?

- What experience do they have that is directly relevant to the opportunity they are pursuing?

- What skills, abilities, and knowledge do they have?

- How realistic are they about the venture's chances for success and the tribulations it will face?

- Who else needs to be on the team?

- Are they prepared to recruit high-quality people?

- How will they respond to adversity?

- Do they have the mettle to make the inevitable hard choices that have to be made?

- How committed are they to this venture?

- What are their motivations?

Components of the Business Plan

Components:

- Executive Summary

- Business Concept

- Founding Team

- Industry/Market Analysis

- Product/Service Plan

- Operations Plan

- Marketing Plan

- Financial Plan

- Growth Plan

- Contingency Plan and Harvest Strategy

- Timeline to Launch

- Append

Mistakes in Developing the Business Plan

- Projecting rapid growth beyond the capabilities of the founding team

- Envisioning a three-ring circus with only one ringleader

- Reporting performance that exceeds industry average

- Underestimating the venture's need for capital

- Mistaking tactics for strategy

- Using price as a market strategy for a product or service

- Not investing in the business

The Look of the Business Plan

- Professional but not slick

- Use index tabs to separate major sections

- Proofread the contents

- Support claims with solid evidence

- Number each copy of the business plan

- Include a Statement of Confidentiality

Physically Organizing the Business Plan

- Cover page for the bound document

- Body of the business plan

- Supporting documents—the appendices

Business Plan Checklist

1. Does the executive summary grab the reader's attention and highlight the major points of the business plan?

2. Does the business plan concept section clearly describe the purpose of the business, the customer, the value proposition, and the distribution channel and convey a compelling story?

3. Do the industry and market analyses support acceptance and demand for the business concept in the marketplace and define a first customer in depth?

4. Does the management team plan persuade the reader that the team could successfully implement the business concept?

5. Does it assure the reader that an effective infrastructure is in place to facilitate the goals and operation of the company?

6. Does the operations plan prove that the product or service could be produced and distributed efficiently and effectively?

7. Does the marketing plan successfully demonstrate how the company will create customer awareness in the target market and deliver the benefit to the customer?

8. Does the financial plan convince the reader that the business model is sustainable—that it will provide a superior return on investment for the investor and sufficient cash flow to repay loans to potential investors?

9. Does the growth plan convince the reader that the company has long-term growth potential and spin-off products and services?

10. Does the contingency and exit strategy plan convince the reader that the risk associated with this venture can be mediated? Is there an exit strategy in place for investors?

INSPIRATIONAL QUOTES TO ENERGIZE YOUR QUEST

KEEP TRYING—Dale Carnegie

"Most of the important things in the world have been accomplished by people who have kept on trying when there seemed to be no hope at all."

YOU CAN DO IT—John Wooden

"Do not let what you cannot do interfere with what you can do."

HANG ON—Franklin D. Roosevelt

"When you come to the end of your rope, tie a knot, and hang on.

BE OPTIMISTIC—Winston Churchill

"The pessimist sees difficulty in every opportunity. The optimist sees the opportunity in every difficulty."

GIVE LIFE YOUR ALL—Walter Cronkite

"I can't imagine a person becoming a success who doesn't give this game of life everything they've got."

POSSIBILITIES—Michael J. Fox

"I see possibilities in everything. For everything that's taken away, something of greater value has been given."

Sole Proprietorship

Main Advantages

- Simple and inexpensive to create and operate

- Owner reports profit or loss on his or her personal tax return

Main Drawbacks

- Owner personally liable for business debt

General Partnership

Main Advantages

- Simple and inexpensive to create and operate

- Owners (Partners) report their share of profit or loss on their personal tax return

Main Drawbacks

- Owner (Partners) personally liable for business debt

Limited Partnership

Main Advantages

- Limited partners have limited personal liability for business debts as long as they don't participate in management

- General partners can raise cash without involving outside investors in management of business

Main Drawbacks

- General partners personally liable for business debts

- More expensive to crate than general partnership

- Suitable mainly for companies that invest in real estate

Regular Corporation

Main Advantages

- Owners have limited personal liability for business debuts

- Fringe benefits can be deducted as business expense

- Owners can split corporate profit among owners and corporation, paying lower overall tax rate

Main Drawbacks

- More expensive to create than partnership or sole proprietorship

- Paperwork can seem burdensome to some owner

- Separate taxable entity

S Corporation

Main Advantages

- Owners have limited personal liability for business debts

- Owners report their share of corporate profit or loss on their personal tax returns

- Owners can use corporate loss to offset income from other sources

Main Drawbacks

- More expensive to create than partnership or sole proprietorship

- More paperwork than for a limited liability company which offers similar advantages

- Income must be allocated to owners according to their ownership interests

- Fringe benefits limited for owners who own more than 2% of shares

Professional Corporation

Main Advantages

- Owners have no personal liability for malpractice of other owners

Main Drawbacks

- More expensive to crate than partnership or sole proprietorship
- Paperwork can seem burdensome to some owners
- All owners must belong to the same profession

Nonprofit Corporation

Main Advantages

- Corporation doesn't pay income taxes

- Contributions to charitable corporation are tax-deductible

- Fringe benefits can be deducted as business expenses

Main Drawbacks

- Full tax advantages available only to groups organized for charitable, scientific, educational, literary or religious purposes

- Property transferred to corporation stays there; if corporation ends, property must go to another nonprofit

Limited Liability Partnership

Main Advantages

- Owners (partners) aren't personally liable for the malpractice of other partners

- Owners report their share of profit or loss on their personal tax returns

Main Drawbacks

- Unlike a limited liability company or a professional limited liability company, owners (partners) are personally liable for many types of obligations owed to business creditors, lenders and landlords

- Not available in all states

- Often limited to a short list of professions

Professional Limited Liability Partnership

Main Advantages

- Same advantages as a regular limited liability company

- Gives state licensed professional a way to enjoy those advantages

Main Drawbacks

- Unlike a limited liability company or a professional limited liability company, owners (partners) are personally liable for many types of obligations owed to business creditors, lenders and landlords

- Not available in all states

- Often limited to a short list of professions

Chapter 14

Realize Your Destiny Living Your Dream

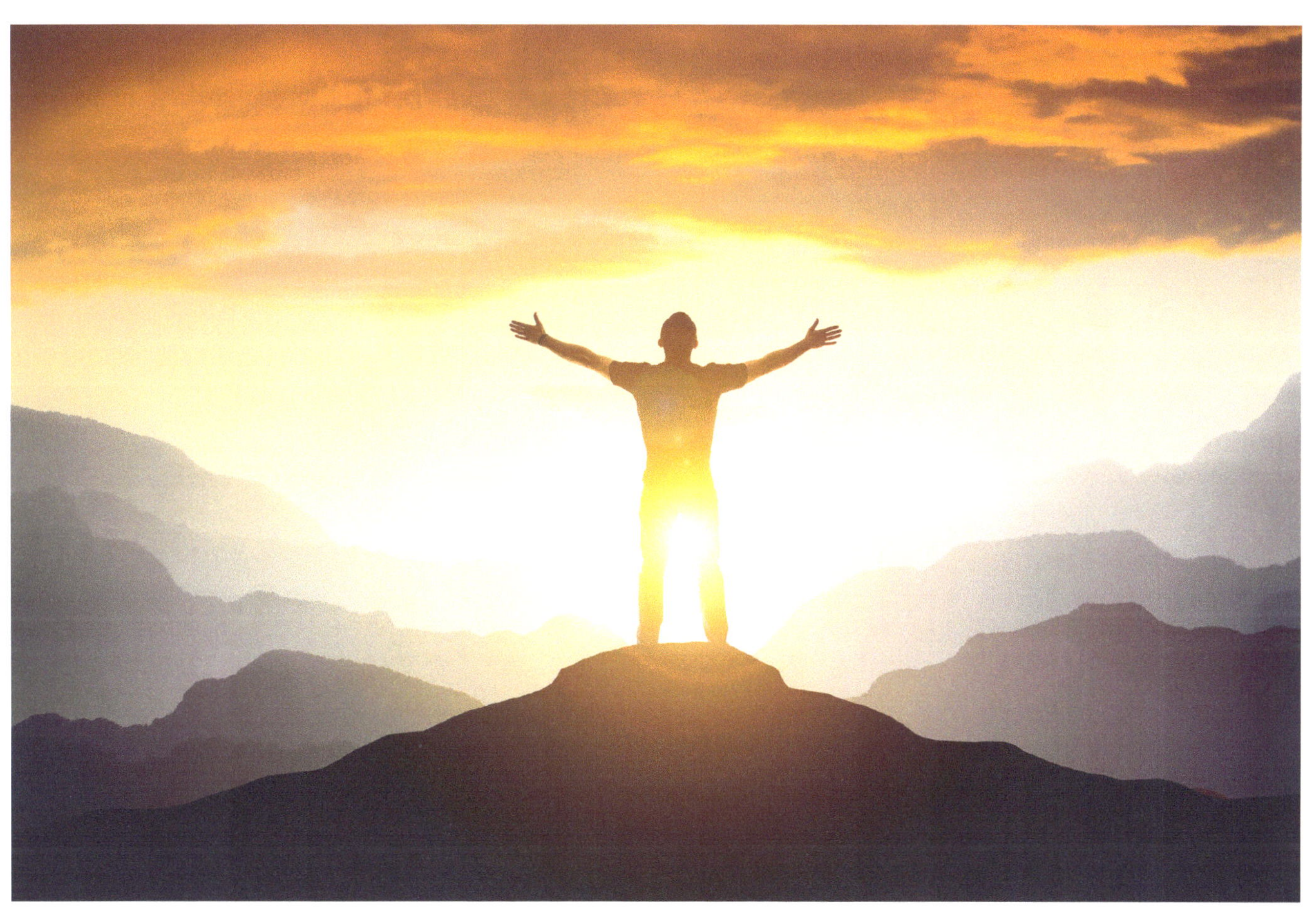

Shutterstock

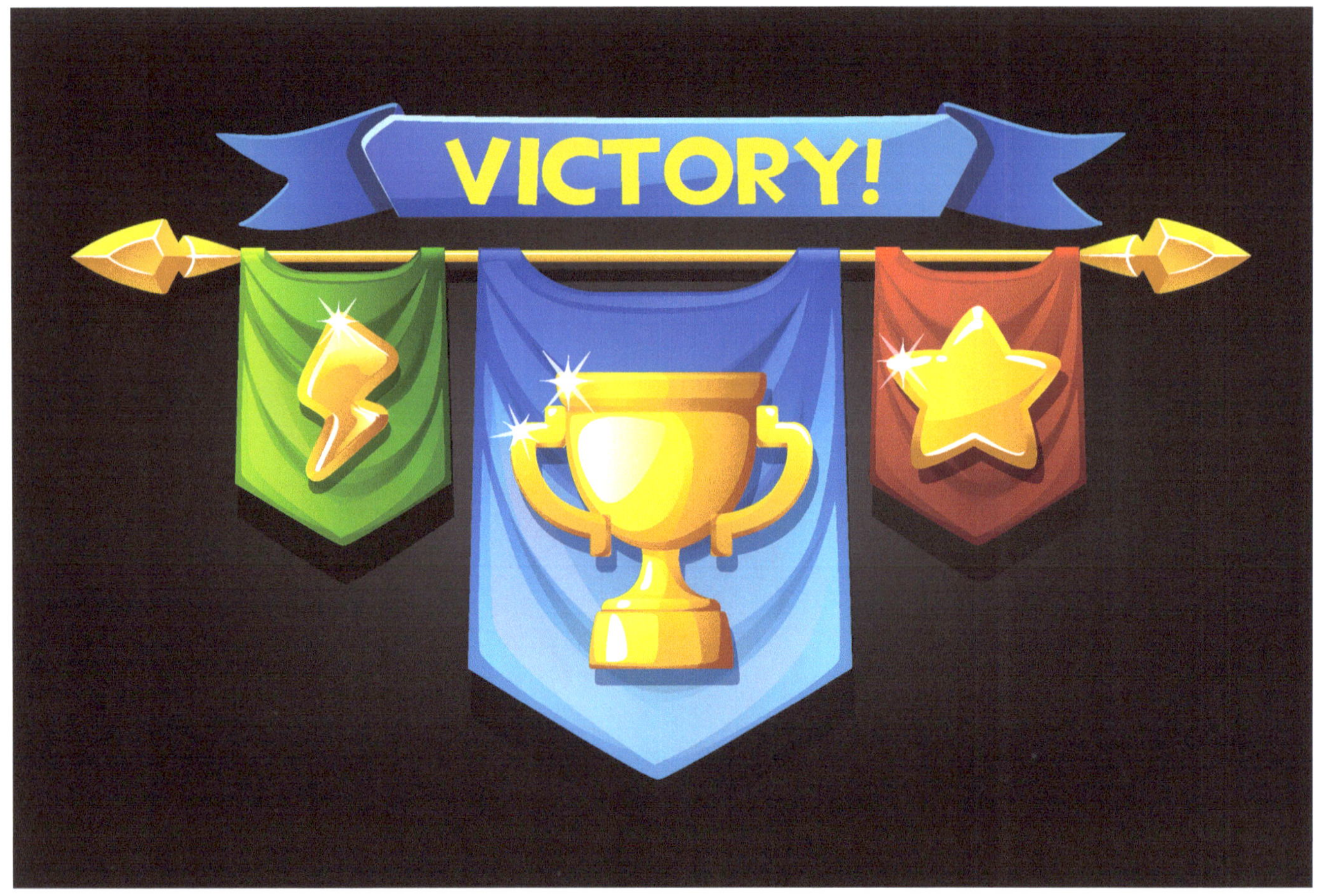

Shutterstock

Do What You Love, Love What You Do. A great trailblazer is made, not born. They are made through training and self-mastery. It is through the exercise of discipline that a person becomes self-regulating. Change happens from the outside in. It is through the expression of courtesy that a person becomes polite. It is through the resistance of fear that a person develops courage. To be the driving force in your dream come true venture, the choices that you make depend on your proven adaptableness to make sound informed decisions and your ability to navigate uncertainty. In addition to adaptability, more than ever respect, and inclusivity are important commander traits to learn for your enterprise.

Talent Isn't Enough

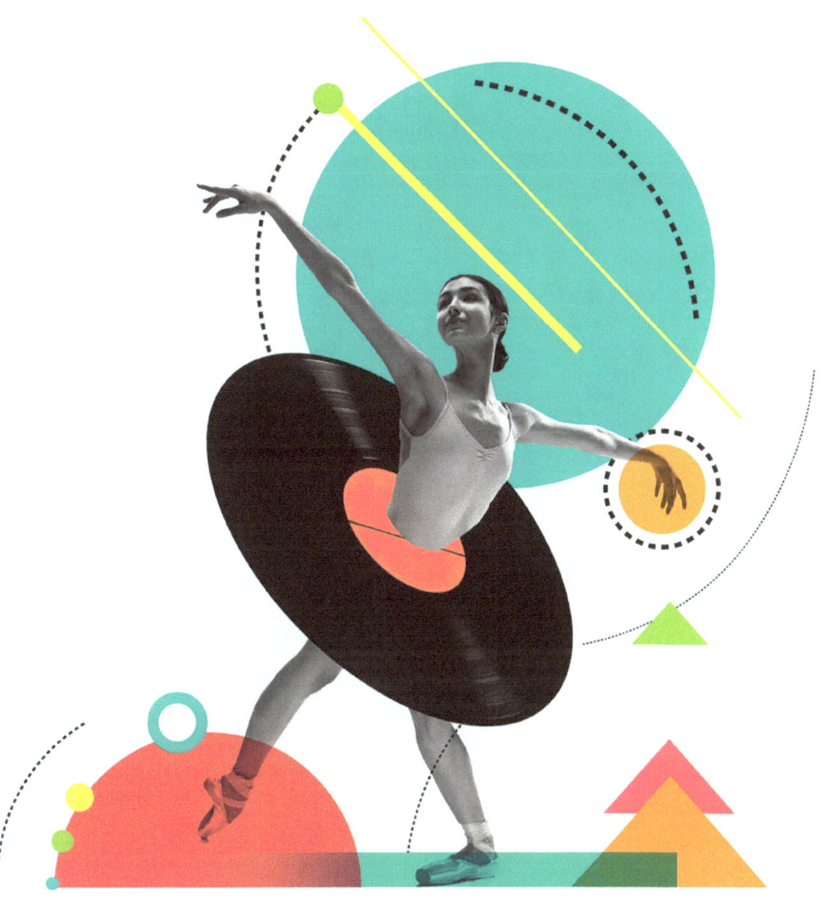

Shutterstock

Success demands a fierce inner fire and drive to persist against all obstacles. The passion to persevere. *"A Great Attitude becomes a great day, which becomes a great month, which becomes a great year, which becomes a Great LIFE."* – Mandy Hale.

When your enterprise invests in employees, support, and social connections, it leads to enhanced performance. You'll be happier. That happiness and optimism and social connections are exactly what's going to fuel sales to hit your sales targets.

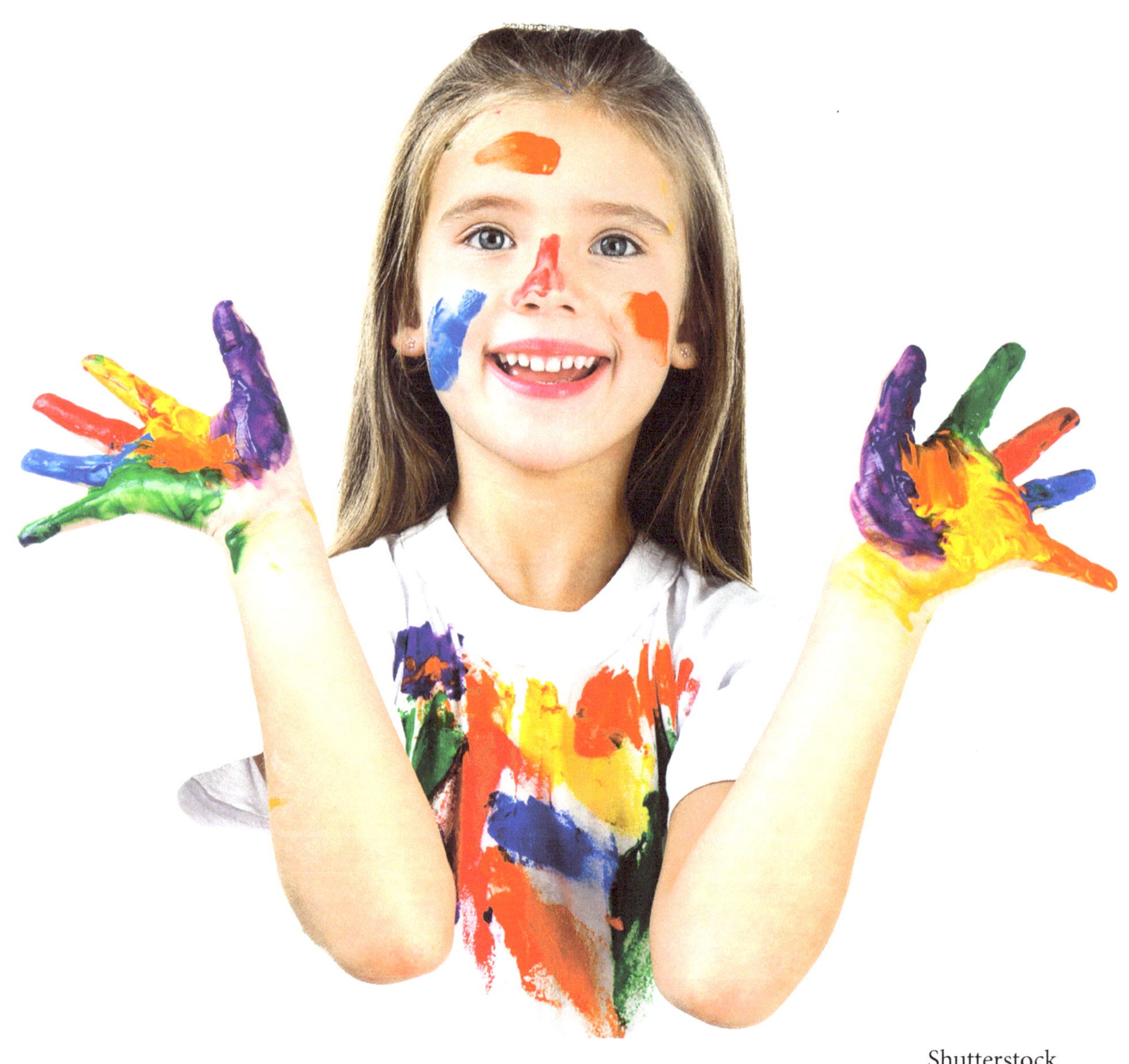

Shutterstock

Making A Living

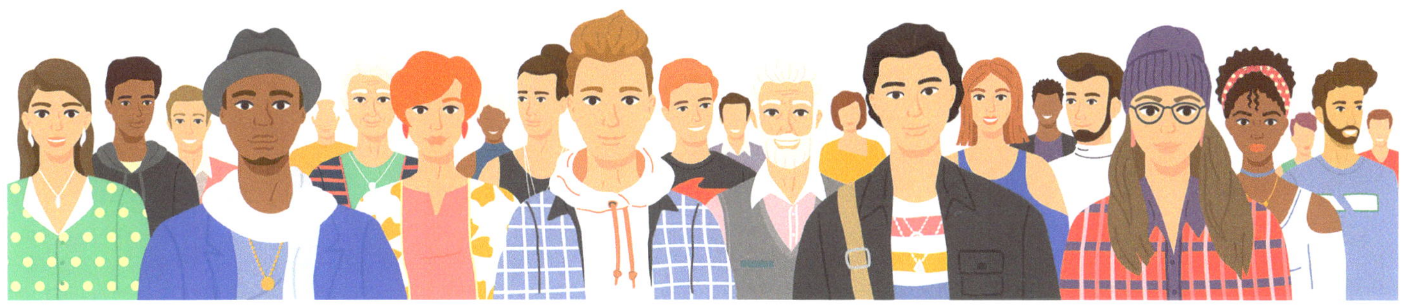

Shutterstock

Build a staff of likable human beings who work well with each other. Show them emotional intelligence that helps them understand the way people feel and react by recognizing and encouraging other people's talents. Sometimes it seems that only ruthless bullies make it to the top of the business ladder, but that's not always the case. Of course, there will always be oppressive managers.

Loving Your Job

Love your work. At no time accept a mediocre work ethic in yourself or employees. Coach your team exactly how to be a valuable human resource. And always make ample time for them to do their assignments exactly right. Count on their most excellence performance.

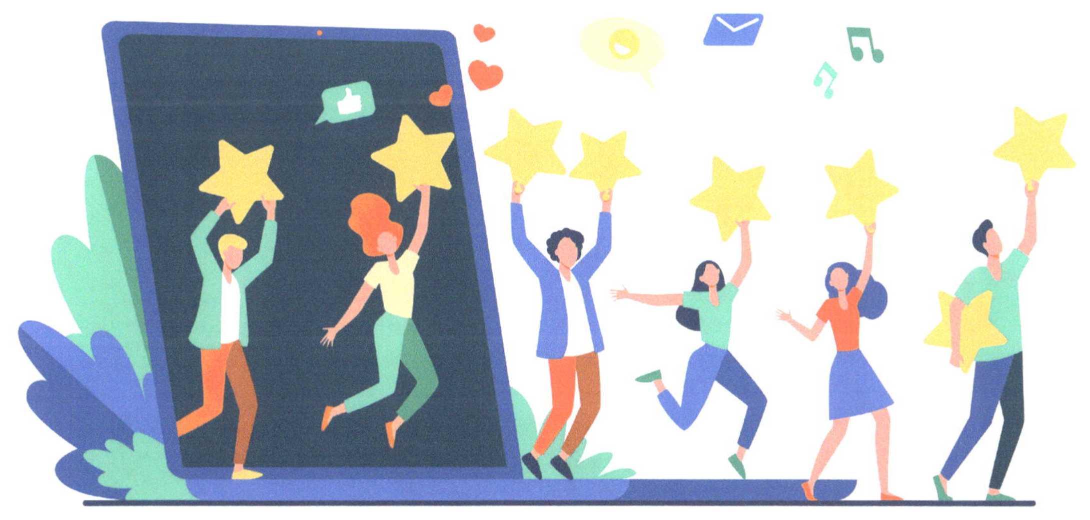

Shutterstock

When your team feels socially connected and supported, and they feel that their work is consequential, they feel more optimistic. When they come to view stress as not a threat but a challenge, their productivity rises dramatically.

Respect

There are two main ways people motivate themselves—through self-criticism or through self-comparison. Self-criticism is being hard on yourself or scaring yourself with the fear of failure. But for people who self-criticize, failure can be scary. Self-compassion on the other hand is a form of motivation that accesses the brain and body's "care systems," the ones we tap into when helping fellow employees through hard times. Self-compassion is about learning to be kind to oneself when things don't work out and recognizing that nearly all successful people struggle through setbacks.

Social support is a great predictor of happiness more than any other factor. Rather than success leading to happiness, the reverse is true: happiness leads to success.

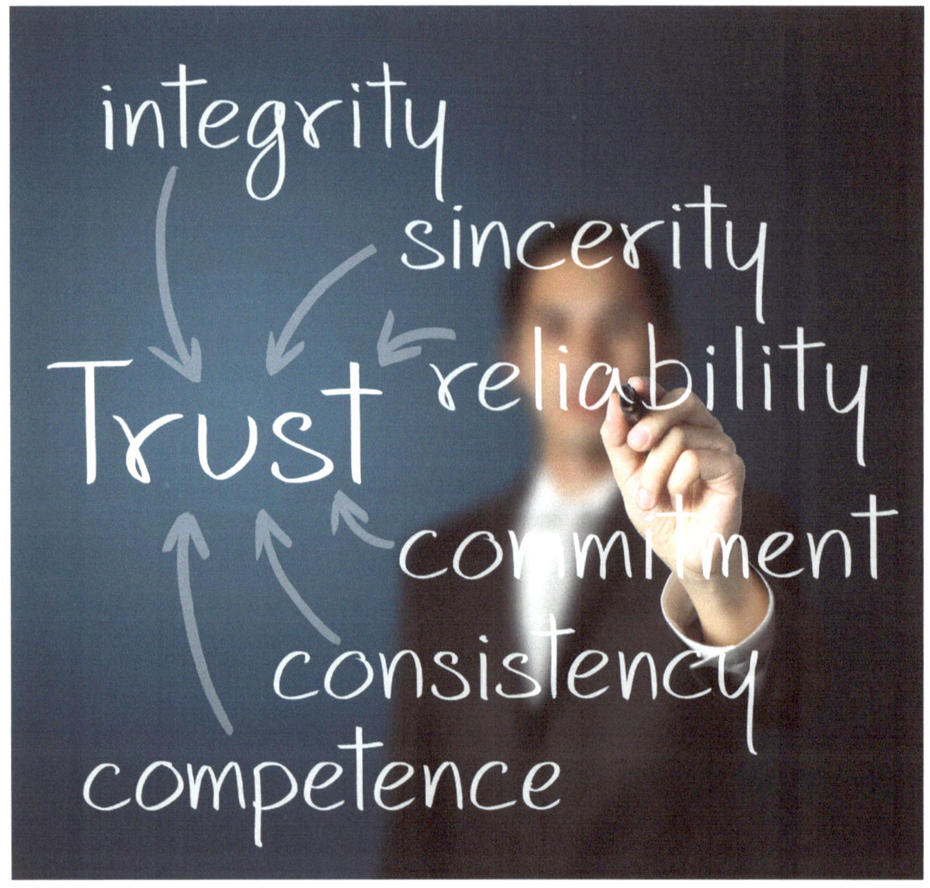

Shutterstock

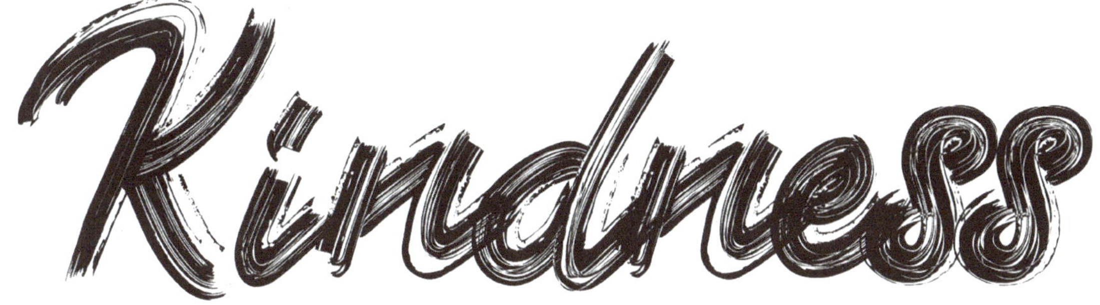

Kindness

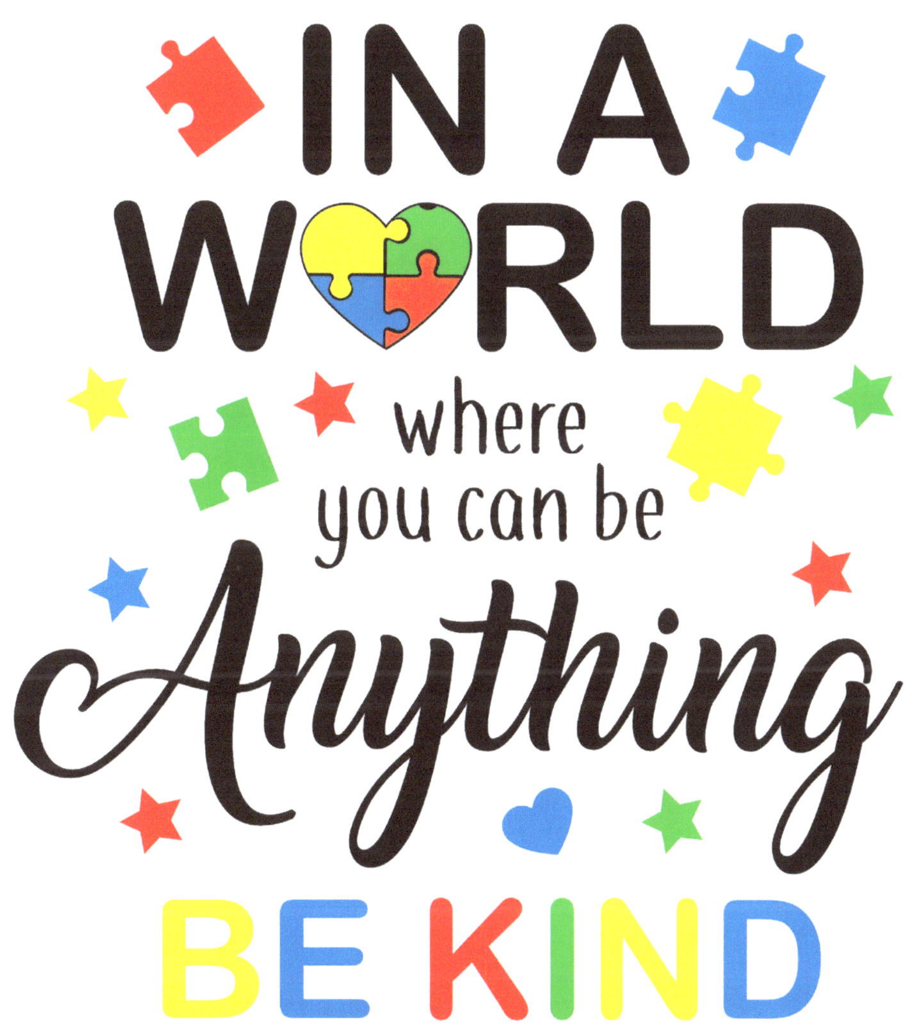

IN A
WORLD
where
you can be
Anything
BE KIND

Helping others plays in your own success. We live in a world dominated by collaboration. The ability to make a group more than the sum of its parts and to establish a meaningful connection with other people—those skills matter more and more.

Cre8ives have a drive to create. They like making stuff. Their passion is enduring. The highly successful have a kind of ferocious determination of passion and perseverance that makes them high achievers and hardworking. They know in a very deep way what it is they want. They not only have determination, but they also have direction. It is this combination of passion and perseverance that makes high achievers special; they have a gift.

A factor in one's level of achievement is not simply genetics or innate talent but deliberate practice of a particular skill. A primary predictor of creative achievement is how much time the individual spends engaged in the activity. Hard work is essential to achieving success.

For those aiming to achieve in the creative realm, the primary predictor of creative achievement is the sheer number of attempts. Successful poets write more poems, successful inventors claim more patents, successful scientists publish more journal articles. Only a small proportion of those poems, patents, or articles will actually carry the weight of the creator's success.

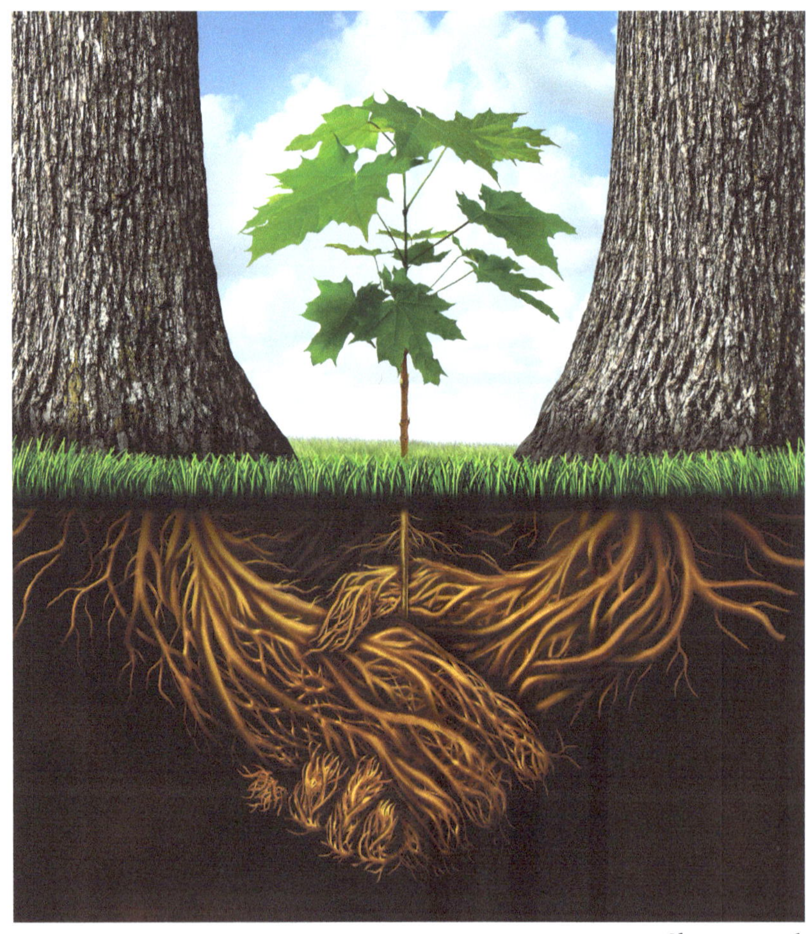

Shutterstock

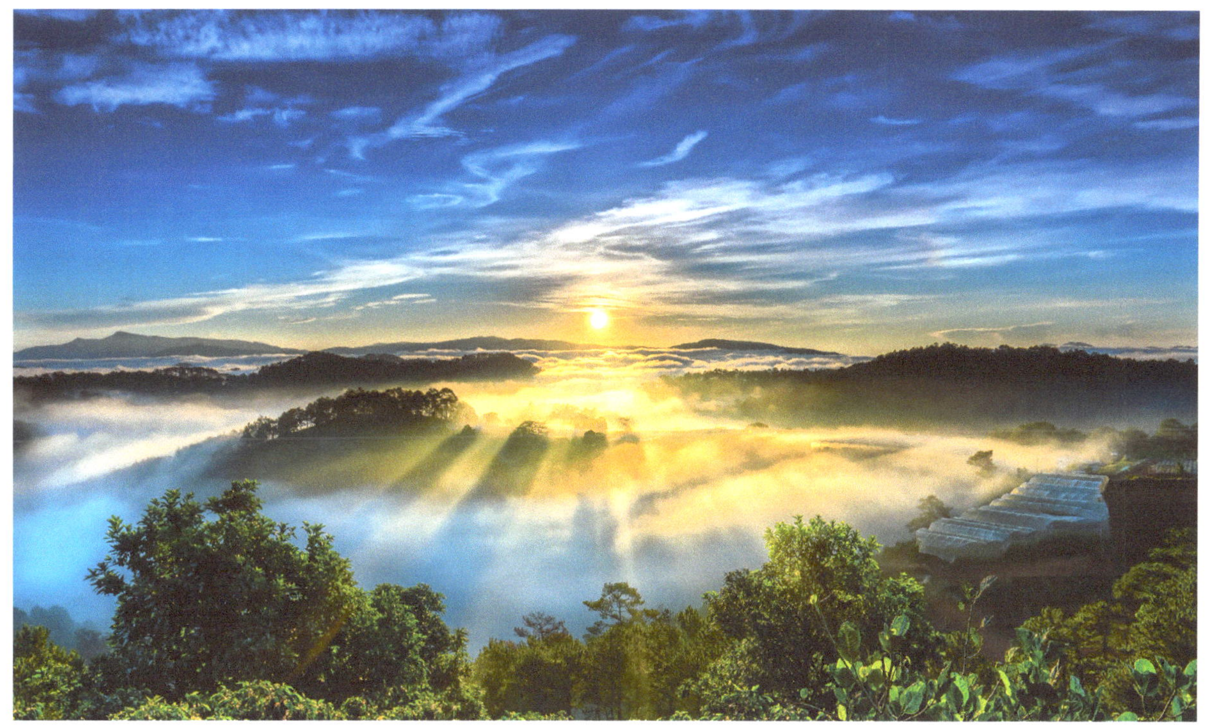

Shutterstock

Running with Gazelles, Eating with Lions
—African Proverb

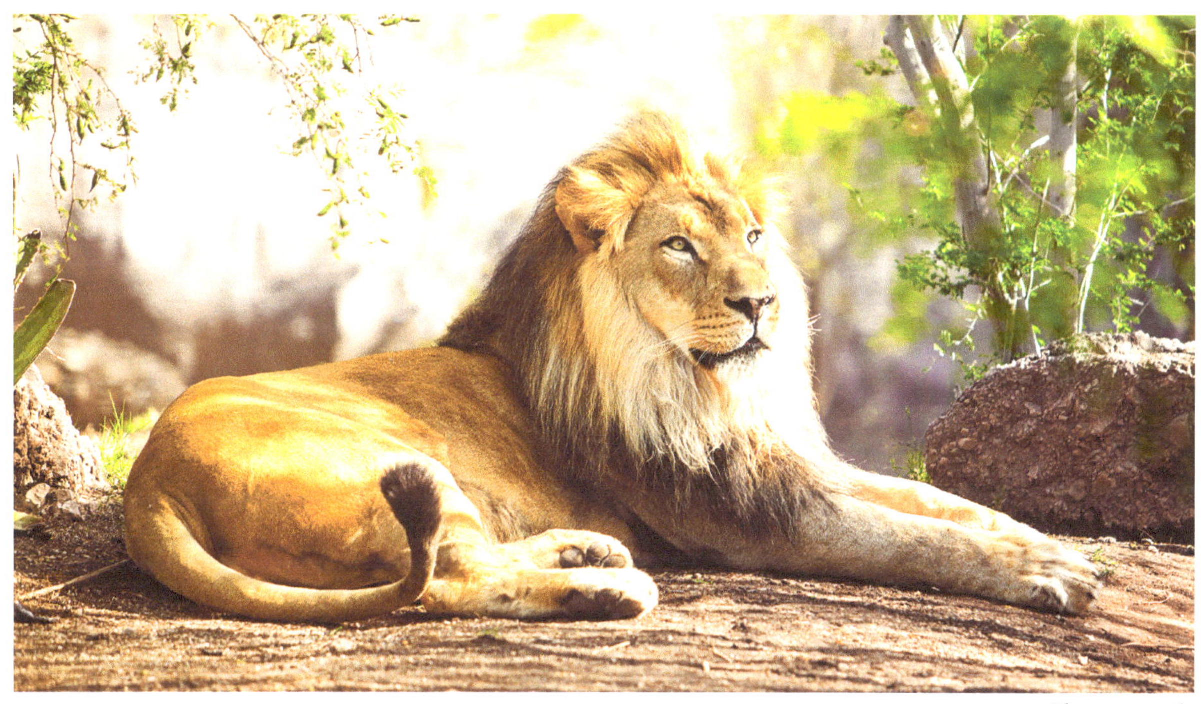

Shutterstock

Every morning, a lion wakes up.

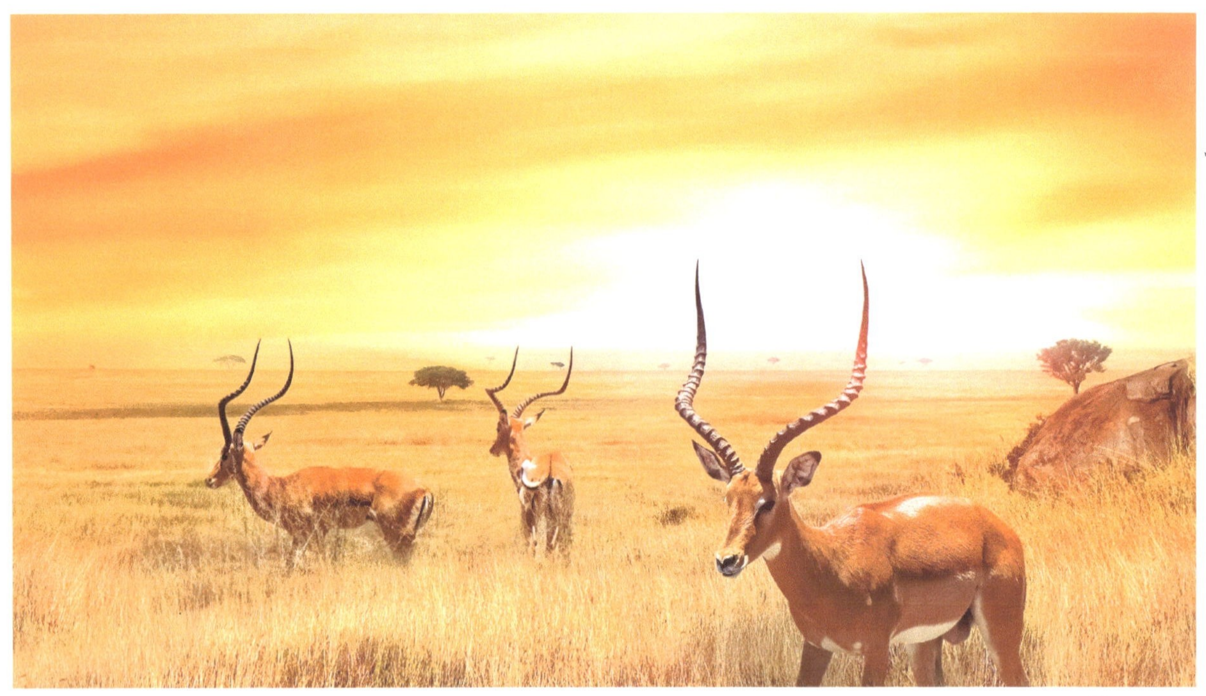

Shutterstock

Every morning in Africa, gazelles wake up.

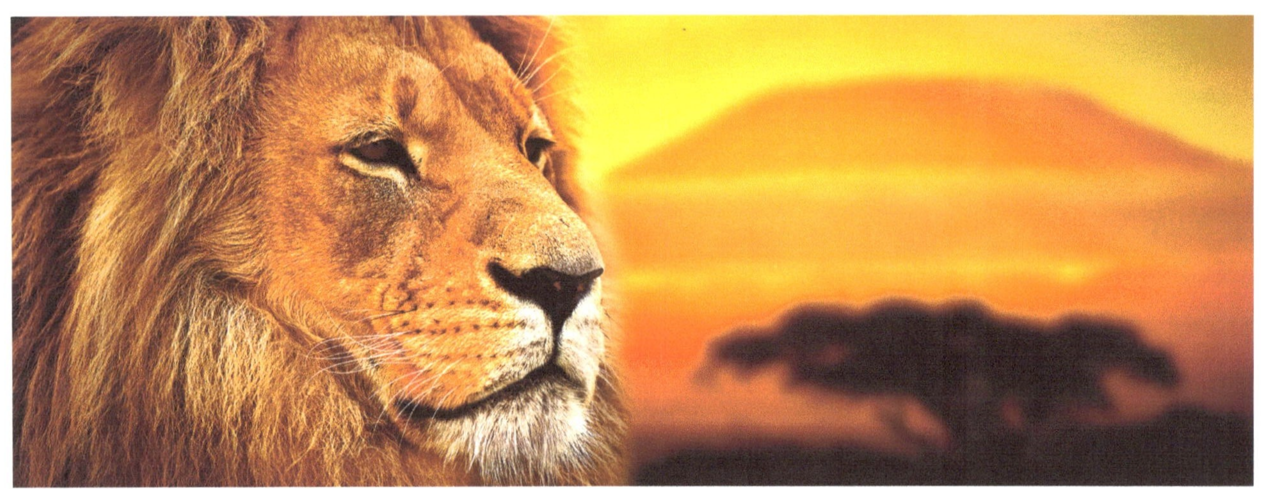

Shutterstock

The lion knows it must outrun the slowest gazelle, or it will starve to death.

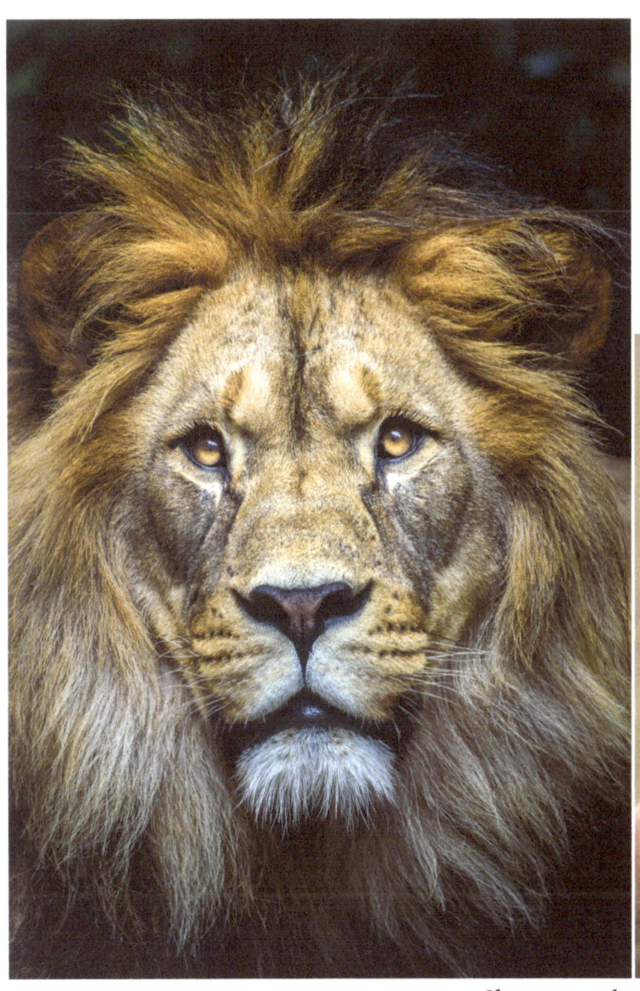

Shutterstock

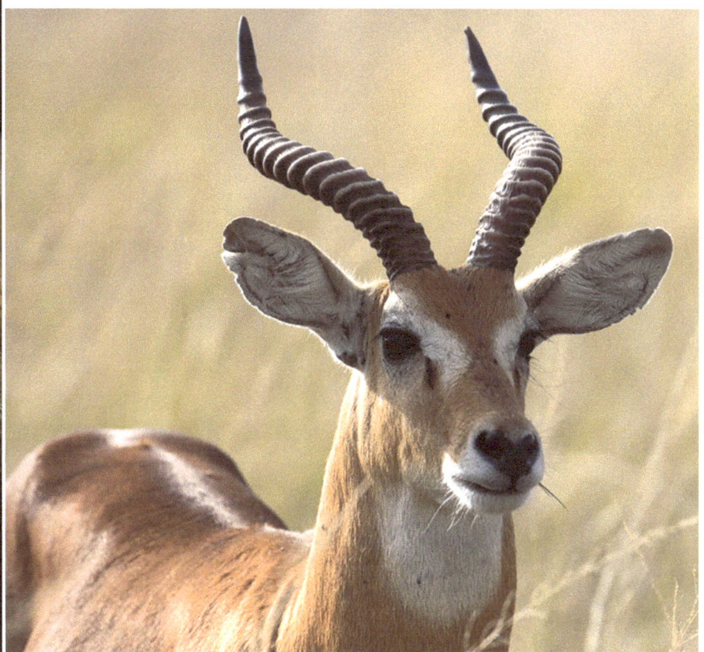

Shutterstock

It doesn't matter whether you are a lion or a gazelle.

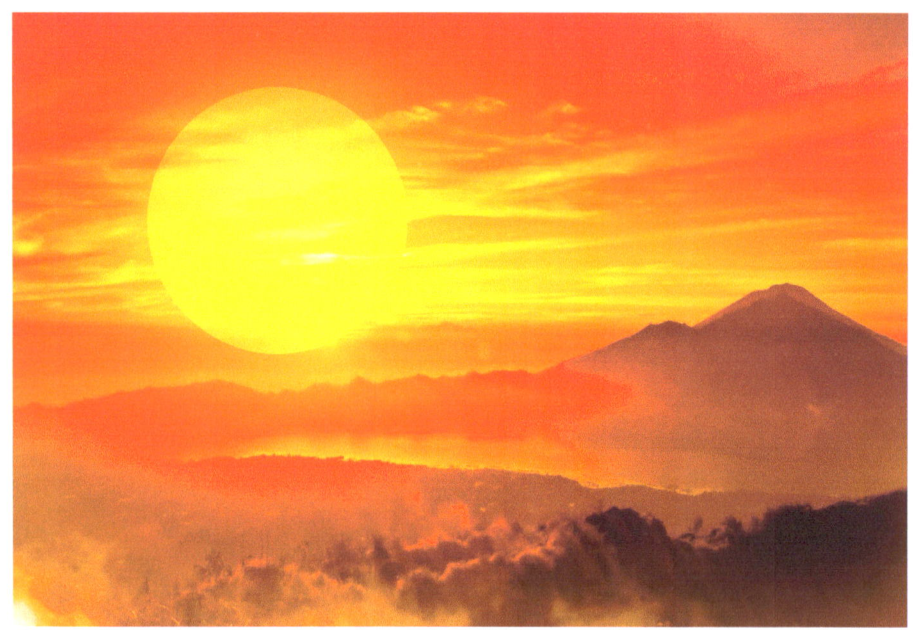

**When the sun comes up,
you had better start running.**

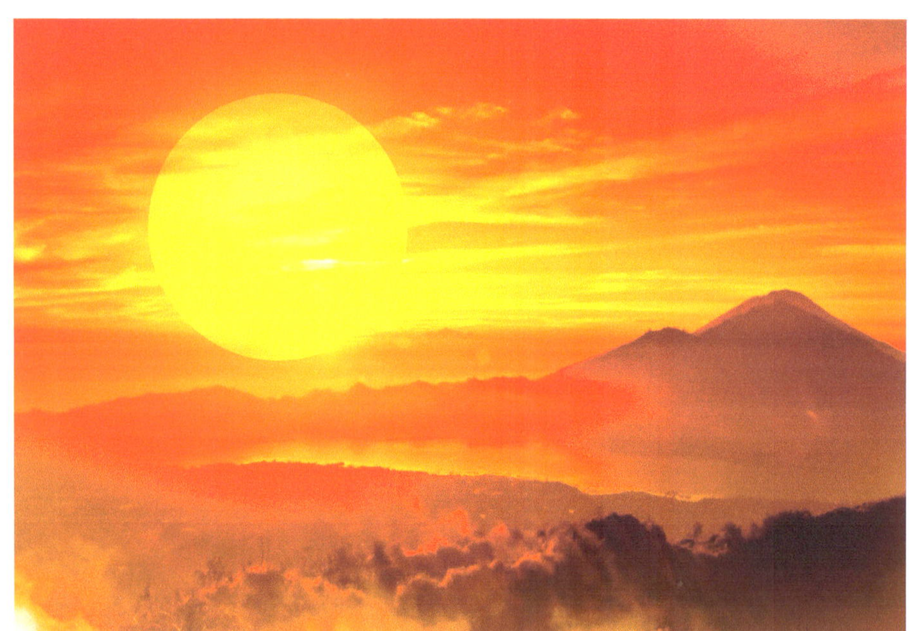

**"You can't build a reputation on
what you're going to do." —Henry Ford**

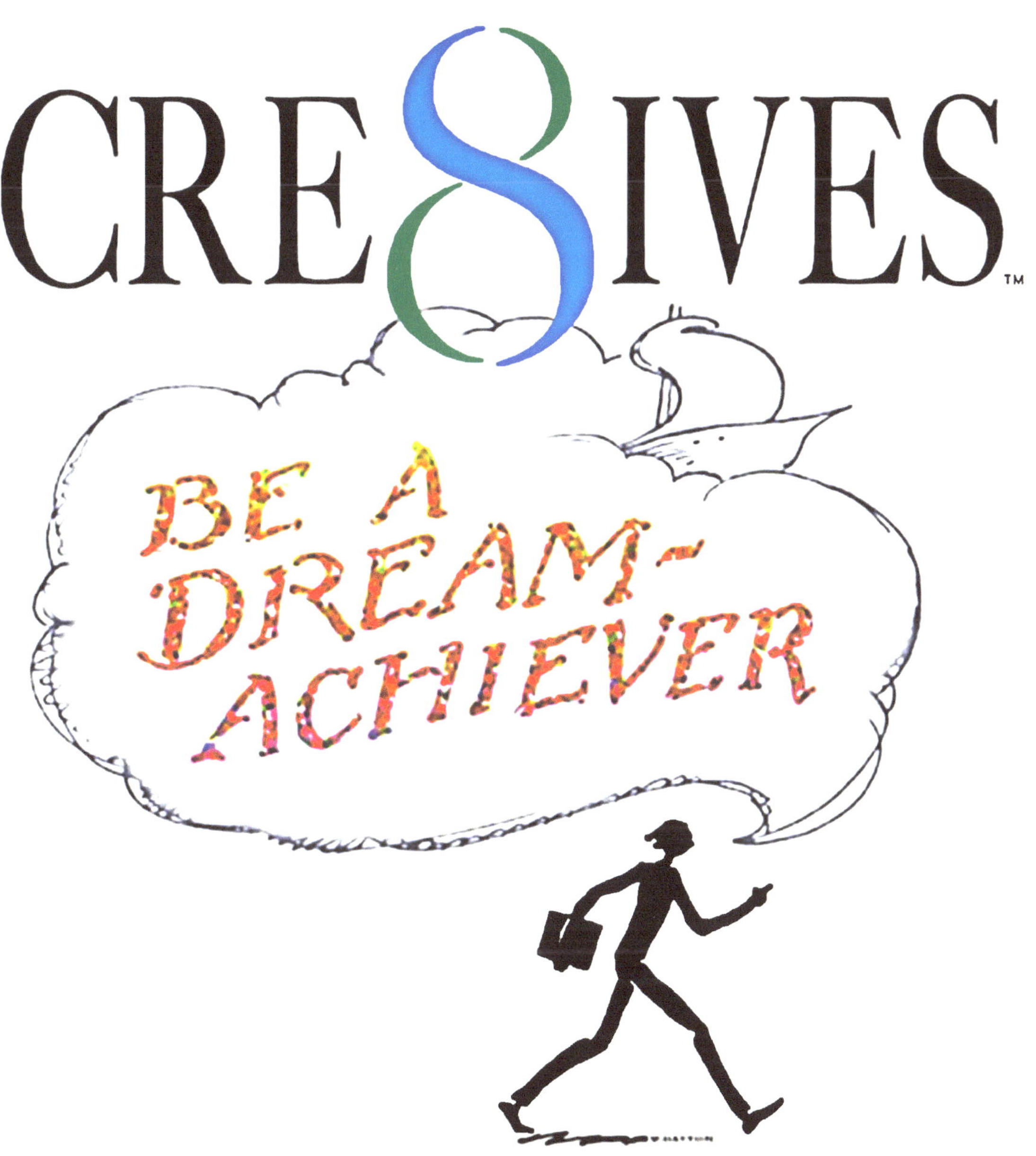

Warren Dayton

I was a Guide 1 / Cultural Interpreter for 8 years at Hearst Castle, the third most visited House Museum in America. William Randolph Hearst was a dreamer and doer. Born into a family of great wealth, he was the only child of George and Phoebe Hearst. George was a gold-miner-owner. In 1880 he bought the San Francisco Examiner, to launch his career in politics. He became a U.S. Senator from California serving from 1886–91.

William attended Harvard University for two years. He became interested in journalism serving as a business manager of the *Harvard Lampoon*. After discontinuing his education at Harvard University, his dad offered him the opportunity to take over the San Francisco Examiner. William jumped for joy and said yes to his father's offer. William remade the paper into a blend of reformist investigative reporting and colorful sensationalism. Within two years, the Examiner was showing a profit.

By 1925, William pushed forward to establish or acquire newspapers in every section of the United States, as well as several magazines. With the help of his mother Phoebe and the family fortune, he went on to become America's first media mogul. He also published books of fiction, owned radio stations, produced the Hearst Metrotone News for movie theaters and motion pictures featuring actress Marion Davies. Hearst had his way because of the reach of his media empire.

There have been a lot of rumors regarding William's record at Harvard. On January 11, 1932, in a Letter to the Editor William defends his Harvard record. *"I was not expelled in '87 nor any other year. I never did anything very bad at Harvard nor anything very good either. I was rusticated in '86 for an excess of political enthusiasm and a certain deficiency in intellectual attainments. I did not return to be graduated. There did not seem to be either reason or hope. I think the less said about my college career the better. Perhaps that is so with the rest of my career. However. Exercise your own judgment. Only please print the facts, or perhaps I should say, please don't."*

William's father, with his great wealth from his mining enterprise, established a 97,000-acre working cattle ranch on the central coast of California, mid-way between Los Angeles and San Francisco. George would always say one thing about the ranch, "I'm saving it for the boy."

Willy, as his dad called him, and his dad would stay in tents on a hilltop they called Camp Hill. The view of the Pacific Coast was spectacular. Camp Hill became the site of William's boundless ambition. The Castle he built there was grandiose. Hearst Castle today is a historic, palatial estate known formally as La Cuesta Encantada (Spanish for "The Enchanted Hill"). Conceived by William and his architect Julia Morgan, the Castle was built between 1919-47. Today, Hearst Castle is a museum open to the public as a California State Park and registered as a National Historic Landmark and California Historical Landmark. William furnished his residential complex with a vast collection of antiques and art objects that he had bought in Europe.

In the here and now, the Hearst family-owned Hearst Corporation is still one of the largest media enterprises in the United States, with global interests in magazines and broadcasting.

My study of William Randolph Hearst's life has taught me . . . DREAMS are meant to be shared because it is only by sharing dreams that they live on. It doesn't look back and think about what might have been but looks forward to what might be. Follow your heart and build your dream into reality.

CPSIA information can be obtained
at www.ICGtesting.com
Printed in the USA
BVHW011931140223
658501BV00002B/2